From DRY BONES

From

DRY BONES

Reflections on an Unpredictable Life

To Nick & Patricia
With deep thanks
Peter Moore

PETER MOORE

Library of Congress Control Number: 2013911555
ISBN: Hardcover 978-1-4836-6031-8
Softcover 978-1-4836-6030-1
Ebook 978-1-4836-6032-5

This book was printed in the United States of America.

Rev. date: 08/07/2013

To order additional copies of this book, contact:
Xlibris LLC
1-888-795-4274
www.Xlibris.com
Orders@Xlibris.com
132207

CONTENTS

FOREWORD

WHY ON EARTH would one write his (or her) memoirs? Isn't it an exercise in sheer narcissism? Modesty would argue for leaving the story be. For this reason I hesitated to put my life story onto paper, lest I be accused of self-absorption.

But then the thought occurred: Might my children, and even grandchildren, be interested in reading the story at some point? My father had written a brief record of his own heritage, and while my children showed no great interest in it, I certainly did. I recall many a rainy afternoon at my grandparents' house pouring over pictures of distant ancestors encased in faded sepia photographs while my grandmother regaled me with the saga of her own bizarre family.

Then a further thought occurred: Perhaps longtime friends who feature at one or another stage of my life might be curious to see the whole story in which they played a key role. As I read brief portions of this manuscript to a few of them, it seemed as if they were genuinely interested—or perhaps they were just being nice? Nevertheless, I couldn't shake the thought that the story was worth sharing with a wider public.

One or two good friends read the whole manuscript, and confirmed my feeling that the story should be told. Thankfully, they offered some constructive criticisms that I was able to incorporate into the final version here.

But it was another thought that finally pushed me over the line. This is not just a biography or autobiography. It is a story of a young man touched by God's Spirit. Somehow, mysteriously as I think back to those early days, a seed was planted in my soul that developed into full-fledged faith. Consequently unlike many who come to faith in later years, I did so as a young man. My view, then, of high school, college, graduate school, early professional life and so on was colored in a certain way. By no means did I view it through rose-colored glasses. Quite the opposite. My vision was colored by a critical eye that, apart from grace, would probably have turned me into a first class prig.

In the unraveling of my life—and at times it truly unraveled—I discovered that people don't fall *from* grace. We fall *into* grace. Again and again, I discovered in a life of extensive travels, moves from New England to Canada to the Midwest to the Deep South, innumerable personal encounters, and exciting adventures that God was there already, long before I was conscious of Him.

So, my hope is that this is a testimony to God's surprising work, reaching into the life of a generally typical suburban kid, and releasing unexpected gifts that would advance His own reputation. That is certainly my hope for this book.

One final caveat: This is neither a rags-to-riches story nor a silver spoon to a wooden spoon story. Life has been enormously pleasant on the whole. But I make no effort to disguise the pain that a sensitive, overweight, sugar-addicted kid felt in growing up. I hope to show how insignificance and brokenness need not be a life sentence. Thanks to a caring Protector, even a marginalized boy can actually become a man.

The title evokes the story found in Ezekiel chapter 37. As a teenager I belonged to an Octet of boys who sang a number of old spirituals and romance songs *a capella.* My favorite was "Ezekiel connected dem dry bones." Somehow, 50 years after a performance was recorded on a rudimentary tape recorder, a copy fell into my possession. Even though I hear myself singing off key in the background, it remains a treasured possession among the many songs on my iPod.

Post-World War II suburbia was filled with dry bones. It had all the appearance of substance and significance. But it lacked meaning and it failed to satisfy a searching young boy. In my quest, which I set out here, I found that meaning by taking a road less traveled.

While my dry bones were being re-enfleshed, I must have at times looked skeletal to others. But amid many twists and turns, I had discovered purpose and had a mission. This story is the unfolding of that mission.

I'On, Mt. Pleasant
South Carolina

CHAPTER 1

ROOTS

AN AWAKENING REALIZATION

One's own childhood is painful enough. Why try to imagine someone else's? But when the childhood is a close relative's, or a good friend's, it may just turn out to be a tad more interesting. In the case of relatives it is interesting because geneticists say that we have more of our ancestors in us than we sometimes want to admit. That was certainly true in my case. Having thought myself totally different from my father (and mother, for that matter), I realized later in life that I was a lot more like them than I had thought. We mimic our parents in ways both little and big, and much as we sometimes try to shake the continuity we inherit from generations past, the apple really doesn't fall far from the tree.

Consider, for example, a painful incident that I recall from my early 20's—one that my Dad most surely had forgotten decades before he succumbed to galloping leukemia at 92. My Dad had given me a small, green Volkswagen bug. What he was doing with it I have no idea, because he was 6 feet 6 inches tall, weighed about 250, and couldn't have fit into it if he tried. Anyway, it was now mine, and for some reason I was driving into the entrance of the Manursing Island Club—a sybaritic watering hole in Rye, New York. I caught sight of him as he was driving out. We recognized each other and so we stopped for a few words, there being no other cars going either way on the little roadway that led through a large marsh of tall reeds.

Dad asked me if I was taking care of the car. This was one of his obsessions; if he was not washing and waxing a car himself, he was darned sure that someone else was properly maintaining his cars.

"Oh, yeah," I said. "Well, I haven't looked under the boot in a while (the engine of the much-loved and much-mourned bug was in the rear), but it seems to be running OK." That wasn't good enough for my perfectionist father, who then gave me a short lecture on the care of cars, as if I didn't know a thing. Humiliated for all of my 28 years and my blue chip education, I drove off thinking: "Who the heck is he to lecture me on the care of an automobile? He thinks I know nothing." To be honest, he was partly right. It could be argued that I've made a study of *not* knowing much about the inner workings of cars; but I did know enough then to feel demeaned, shamed, and belittled. But that's one small example of life as the son of a perfectionist who still felt he could lecture his adult children on the proper care of their own possessions.

Dad was a big, ungainly guy, but very careful about details. His handwriting said it all: tiny, precise, carefully etched, neat as a pin. That one fact revealed an obsession with the small things of life that governed the way my brother, Eric, and I were raised. We were, of course, terrified of this giant who lived with our mother. His huge hand could leave quite a sore spot on our wet behinds when, in our early years, we misbehaved during our Saturday night bath ritual.

He also had a habit of creeping up the stairs after all the downstairs lights were turned out at night, making macabre, gurgling Frankenstein sounds under his breath that would send shivers up our spines—though we loved it. Of course I had to reproduce this silly little performance for our own children years later. But, let's go back to my father's perfectionism. Stupid mistakes we made at the dinner table came in for swift rebukes, as did poor performance in fulfilling the list of chores to be done on a summer's day before we were free to tear off on our bikes to see friends. Dad once said, half humorously: "I don't make mistakes," and you can be sure we never let him forget that slip of the tongue.

EMITTING EMOTIONS

Fortunately, despite his perfectionism and his gargantuan size, Oscar Moore had a good sense of humor, and allowed himself to be teased by all of us, Mom included. This created a domestic atmosphere where there was a lot of laughter, along with not a few tears. In fact, there was no shortage of emotion in the Moore household. Giving vent to our emotions I think gave us all a secure feeling that once out in the open, those emotions would no longer linger inside and lead to destructive habits or a low self-image. They also gave us a misleading feeling of normalcy as a family that led to a sense that we were pretty typical of the families we knew—perhaps even a bit better. How wrong we were.

But where did this Olympic-sized man come from? His parents, my paternal grandparents, had both died by the time I was two or three, so I have no recollection of them at all. Perhaps they knew me as a baby, but that was the extent of it. My father's mother, I learned, was a dignified, soulful lady with an entrepreneurial streak. Not beautiful, though "handsome" as one used to say, she nonetheless raised her two children (my Dad and his sister, the one I always knew as Aunt Peggy), to value education, do well in life, and think beyond themselves. She was married to an Episcopal clergyman of a distinctly broad church stripe. The Rev. Oscar Moore, my grandfather, was quite a debonair fellow as the photos indicate—a thoughtful, pleasant, inoffensive clergyman with a scholarly temperament and an ability to delight, especially the ladies of his congregations. He would drive around in his horse and buggy, with his little daughter Peg at his side, and drop in for tea with the womenfolk of the parish. Were these just social calls? Who knows?

After graduating from the General Seminary in New York City, my grandfather began his ministry at historic Trinity Church in Newport, Rhode Island. Ultimately he had parishes in Lee, Natick, and Barnstable, Massachusetts. Barnstable was only a summer parish at the time because it was located in what was then a very quiet part of Cape Cod. Early in his career, he was a teacher at St. Mark's School, the prestigious boarding school 25 miles west of Boston that ultimately my Dad, my brother Eric, and I were all to attend—on scholarships. The Rev. Oscar Moore left the faculty of St. Mark's, along with a small group of teachers, to help found Pomfret School in the northeast corner of Connecticut. At some point, he left the world of secondary school teaching to attend seminary and enter the parish ministry. Finally, at the end of his ministry he and my grandmother settled in Dongan Hills, the posh section of Staten Island where he became Rector of St. Andrew's Church. By this time he was getting on in years, and his son, my father, now a young man, was working on Wall Street.

CHURCH AS IT USED TO BE

Unfortunately, my grandfather developed senile dementia. He became forgetful, confused, and disoriented. When my grandfather was unwilling to leave the parish ministry, my father had the unpleasant task of calling on Bishop Manning, the imperious Bishop of New York at the time, who wanted to strike a deal: If my father could persuade his father to leave the parish ministry, the bishop would offer him a decent retirement pension. And that's about all I remember of my grandfather, whose portrait sat for years in a small frame on my bureau. To me he was forever lost in the mists of the past. Dad rarely spoke of him to us. That always made us wonder if Dad was proud of his father. The one story he often did tell us was the time when, at the age of twelve (and already huge for his age), his father told him—in a misguided effort at parental discipline—that he was going to have to spank him. "Up to your room, Oscar, I'm coming to spank you," he said to the young boy. "No, you're not," said Dad, looking his father straight in the eye. From that point on, our Dad had no more to fear from his clergyman father.

His upbringing in the parsonage left my Dad with very mixed feelings about religion. He had more than a casual acquaintance with church ways, having been around clergy and bishops much of his life. But this superficial knowledge led to a mild form of Christianity that may have been vaguely "felt" but was rarely talked about. I recall one year, when, perhaps out of a sense of obligation, he taught Sunday School to seventh graders at our home parish, St. James the Less in Scarsdale. That turned out to be an exercise in futility because whatever content he hoped to communicate was overshadowed by his increasingly desperate efforts at discipline. The recounting of those efforts made for a great deal of merriment around our Sunday dinner table. Fortunately for the children he taught, his career as a Sunday School teacher did not last long.

THE MOORES I BARELY KNEW

My paternal grandmother was a different story. While I have no recollection of her, she seems to have been much loved by her son. Dad particularly admired his mother's entrepreneurial streak. On one occasion she spotted a sign in front of a house in Barnstable on the Cape, announcing that the house was "up for auction". She ventured forth with a tiny inheritance that she had received and, to everyone's surprise, secured the house at a rock bottom price. The sizeable structure, though not particularly attractive by present-day standards, became the family's summer cottage for years. Her opportunistic gamble established her as a lady of substance and vision, as well as a gracious hostess.

On the Moore side of the family, I came to know few relatives personally. One, however, was Uncle Ed Bayles, brother of my grandmother, another very tall man who had married "well" as we used to say. His wife, Aunt Madeleine Gould, was the beneficiary of a considerable inheritance that enabled the two to live comfortably in Orange, New Jersey. When Uncle Ed died, having no children, he divided his own estate between a hospital in Orange and his sister's two children, my Dad and his sister, Peggy. Although it was not a large amount of money, it did enable both Dad and Aunt Peggy to augment their incomes in such a way that in later life they were able to afford many nice things that had been denied them in their early married lives. It was some 50 years later, when our Dad died, that my brother Eric and I inherited the same stocks that our Dad had carefully guarded all those years. They provided us with a little nest egg. However, the money arrived long after it might have proved useful to us in raising our families.

By a series of strange coincidences, I managed to get to know Uncle Ed Bayles' widow, Aunt Madeleine. Many women on both sides of my family were named Madeleine; it must have been a popular girl's name in the nineteenth and early twentieth centuries, and may even be staging a come back. Aunt Madeleine and Uncle Ed had retired from the Oranges to their summer home in Dennis on Cape Cod, and long after Uncle Ed had died I would visit her there from time to time—even using her home as a retreat. The place, now sadly derelict, had a delightful gazebo encased in glass right on the edge of Scargo Lake. It was there, as a single young clergyman, that I could quietly read and write, while Aunt Madeline's cook and chauffeur took care of my creature comforts.

She took particular interest in the birds outside her sun porch, and had the habit of sending the chauffeur on many a trip to obtain "fresh" coffee ice cream, one of her several indulgences.

Again on the Moore side of my family, there was Uncle Fred. Fred Bayles, another sibling of my grandmother Moore's, lived in St. Louis, where one branch of the Bayles clan had settled. He was either widowed or a bachelor (the latter, I think), and he would occasionally come east and stay with us. He was the kind of elderly uncle every little boy enjoys. He had a twinkle in his eye, was easy to be with, and seemed endlessly inventive. One day my brother and I, both quite little, were taking a bath together and we were unable to turn off the water in the tub. As the water kept rising to dangerous heights, Eric and I desperately tried to turn the faucet off. Uncle Fred happened to be staying with us, and he dashed up the stairs, quietly took the faucet handle and totally unwound it almost to the very end. Then he deftly re-wound it to the point where the water shut off. He somehow knew all about re-threading a faucet, a trick none of us would have dreamed of ourselves. At the time it seemed almost miraculous.

AUNT PEGGY PETERSEN

But it was Dad's sister, Aunt Peggy, whom I really got to know well on his side of the family. She was a large woman, not especially pretty, with strong, bony hands. To my brother and me, she seemed to live a fascinating life. Although very much a New Englander like her brother, she ended up settling in Irving, Texas, where she helped to pay the bills by selling real estate and growing peaches on a mid-size farm. When we were young children, she lived as a divorcee in New York City, and would invite my brother and me to come to the City by train from Scarsdale where we lived and grew up. We anticipated these marvelous adventures with great glee. One time it would be the Central Park Zoo. Another it would be the Museum of Natural History. Always there were visits to Schrafft's, an upscale restaurant, or so it seemed to us, or—even more enticingly—lunch at the Automat.

The Automat, now perhaps forgotten, was a long-time New York institution. One deposited a handful of nickels in little glass boxes on the wall, then a door would flip open and from inside one could draw a sandwich, a piece of pie, a pot of Jell-O, or other wonderful things. To a child the Automat was sheer magic. It was the perfect marriage of technology and food! However, technology killed the Automat, the way video killed the radio star. We loved these visits, and grew to view Aunt Peggy as a purveyor of exotic, exciting experiences.

When we returned home from our New York magical mystery days, we would of course recount our adventures to our parents. "Oh, yes", we would tell them, "and we saw Uncle Ed in the afternoon too." Our parents would at that point exchange knowing glances that were totally incomprehensible to us. What we did not know then, but later learned, was that Aunt Peg had divorced her husband Ed Petersen some years before, but was obviously continuing to see him—or at least she did when we were with her. Eventually she remarried Ed Petersen and together they moved west to Texas to start a new life. There he, a World War II veteran, attempted to make a living selling insurance while she grew peaches and sold real estate.

My brother's and my biggest adventure with our Aunt Peggy came in 1947 when we first boarded an airliner and flew to Dallas to experience the West. I was eleven, and my brother Eric twelve and a half. It was thoroughly enchanting despite my very great disappointment that the plane managed to skirt around (rather than fly through) a number of large cumulonimbus clouds. Later, flying here and there became a familiar event in my life but in 1947 it was full of wonder. During that summer we discovered the rough and tumble of Texas life on the peach ranch.

AN UNFORGETTABLE SUMMER

Texas in July was unbearably hot from our standpoint. Few people had heard of air conditioning in those Spartan post-World War II years. We slept outside in a screened-in sleeping porch and by the time evening came, we'd had enough of the heat. So with Aunt Peg's permission (but not Uncle Ed's) we slipped our less-than-clean pajamas into the deep freeze, which was also located on the porch, so that we could have just a few delectable minutes of cool before retiring for the night. When Uncle Ed discovered our little gimmick, it was abruptly stopped.

That summer lived up to our dreams. There was a trip to West Texas to see a real rodeo and eat from a real chuck wagon. Marvelous. There were mornings at the Dallas farmer's market where I would shout out "freestone or "clingstone" in an effort to sell bushels of peaches to the crowds in search of produce. The first time I tried driving a car was one uncomfortably sultry day when we were out in the peach orchard picking fruit, getting covered all over with itchy peach fuzz. We had run out of water, and someone had to go back to the house to get more. But the house, a rather nicely remodeled chicken coop, was a mile or so away. My Aunt Peggy tossed the keys to her truck in my direction, and said, “Peter, why don’t you drive back and get us some water.” Stunned, I recall saying, “Sure, Aunt Peg, but you’ll have to show me which gear is which.” Back I drove, feeling ten years older than the eleven that I was. My self-image soared to new heights, which was precisely the result she had intended. I proudly returned with the water, having driven the entire way there and back on her dirt road in first gear. Nonetheless, I was now a man, having crossed an essential rite of passage at the tender age of eleven. I will always be thankful to her for that remarkable vote of confidence. Of course, in Texas it would not have mattered if I had traveled on a state road. In those semi-frontier days, Texas had no minimum driving age. It stands to reason that farm boys had to use vehicles for this and that. My experiences only reinforced my image of Texas as a wild and lawless land of infinite possibilities.

During that eventful summer, my brother and I got to know many of Aunt Peg and Uncle Ed’s friends. There was Edith Sinnett, a single woman who had been more or less adopted into their family, and who lived with them for decades. Edith and Peggy had worked together in the Girl Scouts during World War II, and formed a lifelong bond. Then there were the Ganzers, close social friends who would join us for barbecues. One evening, under a Texas moon, I found my tongue loosened, perhaps by some lemonade, and proceeded to tell the Ganzers the whole story of Uncle Ed and Aunt Peg’s divorce and remarriage. They looked stunned, and (can I blame him?) my Uncle Ed was not amused. Apparently, they had never told their best friends of this sad chapter in their lives, and hardly needed me to do the telling for them.

ONE HUNDRED DOLLARS

Two incidents from that eventful summer in the "wilds" of Texas burned themselves into my memory. The first was when Eric and I made injudicious references to the small amount of money that our Dad had entrusted to Aunt Peg to cover our incidental expenses. We had been told that he had forwarded on to her $100 to cover them—real money in those post-War years, but not enough to include our every want and need. However, whenever our desires seemed excessive to Aunt Peg, who after all was *in loco parentis*, we would casually say: "Oh, just take it out of the hundred." Naturally, this grated on and strained our somewhat fragile relationship with her. Our imagined largesse gave Aunt Peg the impression that we were effete Eastern snobs who needed a dose of reality—and she was probably right.

Over the years, Aunt Peg made many trips east and I made several trips west. I became her favorite nephew. She and Eric had gotten off to a rough start somehow, perhaps because Eric was more direct than I was and as the elder nephew felt free to challenge her. It is possible that Eric unwisely repeated some of our Dad's occasional critical remarks about his sister. Following Ed Petersen's death, Peggy and her friend Edith eventually left their beloved Texas for Florida, in order to be closer to our Dad in his retirement. But before she left, she helped found the Irving Symphony, and had a small hand in supporting the University of Dallas, a Catholic college in Irving. Many years later I greatly regretted being unable to fly west to be present for "Peggy Peterson Day" when the Irving Symphony paid special tribute to her vision and energy. As the years wore on, sadly,

Aunt Peg's social drinking developed into an alcohol habit and eventually an alcohol problem. Also, in our Dad's estimation, she was never particularly wise with money. But much of that was invisible to us in our childhood and youth, and her memory remains very special to me. Many readers, who have had beneficent aunts and uncles, will understand. On reflection, I think of her as the first extended family member who believed in me as a person.

CHAPTER 2

THE CHILDRESSES

SOUTHERN HERITAGE

The Childress side of my family, that is my mother's side, was a study in contrast with the Moore/Bayles side. The Childress clan lived all around us in the suburbs north of New York City. Three sets of aunts and uncles, together with their seven children, all grew up close by, which made for great story telling and revelry, especially over Thanksgiving and Christmas dinners.

My grandfather, Avent Childress, had grown up in Murfreesboro, Tennessee, one of three brothers born to a prominent and established, though not especially wealthy, old family. His great aunt, Sarah Childress, had married President James K. Polk, and after the President's death in 1849 she retired to Nashville. A photograph of President Polk and his wife adorned my grandfather's dressing room, and while he rarely spoke of them, it was clear that he was immensely proud of his heritage.

Avent Childress, as the story went, had been dismissed from the Webb School of Bell Buckle. It was a reputable boy's boarding school in rural Tennessee, run by its notorious founding headmaster nicknamed "Sawney" Webb. My grandfather's expulsion went down in family history as the Witch Hazel incident. The hot-tempered and very strict headmaster accused certain boys of using alcohol. This was partially true. Because there were no showers in the gym, the boys had been using Witch Hazel to rub themselves down after sports. However, the smell of alcohol hung heavy in the locker room air, and Webb, who was unfamiliar with the rubbing compound, thought he smelled liquor. The "guilty" boys were immediately dismissed. When my grandfather, who had not been using Witch Hazel himself, openly protested that they had not been drinking, he too was summarily sent home.

But, as the story was told and retold, the Webb School of Bell Buckle was held in such high estimation by universities that along with many of the other boys, my grandfather had no trouble getting into college. Off he went to Princeton, despite his "run-in with the law." He had been the very first lifeguard at the Monteagle summer campground near Sewanee, Tennessee, and was an expert gymnast and very handsome. One day, while swinging on the high bars in the Princeton gym, he caught the eye of my grandmother, a society maiden from New York. They eventually married, and moved to New York City where Avent attempted to make his way in the heady world Wall Street. Eventually they moved to Chappaqua, New York, where my grandmother's father, Donald Mackay, built them a substantial home in which to continue their early married lives adjacent to his extensive estate, Afterglow Farm. The farm burned down many years ago, but some of the adjacent houses still stand, including the one where my grandparents began their marriage. Today the original estate is the property of the Whippoorwill Country Club, and sits atop the highest point in Westchester County.

BOMP

My grandfather was called "Bomp" by all his grandchildren. This was a childlike corruption of Grand-pa; after having been corrupted to ba-pom, eventually ended up as Bomp. He had been raised in the post-Reconstruction South, and reflected the muted racist views of his contemporaries, which drew "Oh, Daddy" comments from his sophisticated daughters, of which my mother was the third of four. He once let it slip that one of his relatives, perhaps even his father, had been instrumental in the founding of the KKK—something that drew embarrassed looks from us all. On a person-to-person level, Bomp could be the soul of kindness to the various Black servants who were hired to help out at large family gatherings, and eventually lived with my grandparents in their latter years. But racism was never far from the surface.

Growing up as fun-loving, slightly lawless grandchildren, accustomed to playing hide-and-seek in the attic during family gatherings, my older cousins and I were of course oblivious to how our occasional trampling through his beloved gardens annoyed our grandfather. So for many years, we all lived in fear of him. On one occasion, when I was about seven, he had left his precious 1939 Buick in front of our house. While he and my grandmother were inside the house visiting with my parents, I at the tender age of three climbed behind the steering wheel, and somehow managed to turn on the ignition, as I had seen him do. To my surprise, with no key at all, the engine started effortlessly, and the Buick and I took off. Barely able to see over the wheel, I was able in just a few minutes to scrape past a fire hydrant, careen across several lawns, demolishing hedges as I went, and end up in the front yard of a neighbor down the road. I recall creeping back into the house and hiding under a large chair while Bomp and my parents assessed the damage. That Buick was one of the last to be built before all automobile construction was halted at the outbreak of World War II, and the factories were pressed into building tanks and other armored vehicles. The Buick was eventually fixed, and nothing more was ever said of the incident.

Avent Childress's values had been shaped by his many years on Wall Street. He survived the boom and bust of the1920's, and recovered from the crash of 1929 to live a relatively comfortable life bringing up his four daughters, sending them by train from Scarsdale to prestigious New York City private girls' schools. None attended college. People with money had always impressed my grandfather, and he measured success in largely materialistic terms. It was a point of pride to him that many of his sons-in-law had attended Ivy League colleges, including my father who played football for Yale in the 1920s. He seemed closer to his other daughters than to my mother (she was number three), a fact which caused her some pain. His two older daughters, whose husbands had been financial successes, seem to have been particularly favored. In my view, he was too easily impressed by clients with sizeable portfolios or large estates, and managed to spend most Saturdays with them on the golf course at St. Andrew's in Ardsley-on-Hudson, or some other swank country club. He appeared to have been blind to his own warped sense of values, but quick to notice the warp in the values of others. He combined an open disdain for others, while at the same time admiring them if they were wealthy. Family members often remembered his off-hand comment about a rich client: "He'd lie down and die for me… the rat."

This over-attentiveness to wealth and social status led my grandfather to misjudge character more than once. Next door to us in Scarsdale lived a childless couple who seemed to have an unsettled relationship. The noise of marital quarrels would occasionally waft across the hedge that separated our two houses. But the husband looked very distinguish and affected an aristocratic bearing. Of him Bomp was once heard to say, "He's a cut above Rugby Lane"—the modest street on which we lived. Not only did that devalue his own daughter and her husband—my parents—but it soon became something of a family joke because my parents had the strong impression that this neighbor was actually trying to murder his wife!

STRICTLY BROOKS BROTHERS

There was a genuinely sweet side to Bomp. Throughout our entire life, all of his grandchildren—male and female—greeted him with a kiss on the cheek and a hug well into our adult years, in fact right up to his death. While he could be very critical of our grandmother, incurring the wrath of his daughters when a cross word was spoken, he had an excellent sense of humor, and took a genuine interest in what family members were doing. Since tennis and paddle tennis, officially known as Platform Paddle Tennis, had become major family sports, I can still picture him at one or another club, dressed in his Brooks Brothers' tweed jacket and bow tie, brimming with pride as he watched his daughters (and grandchildren) make off with trophies and titles. He was more than usually attentive to his appearance, watched his weight very carefully, and looked perpetually handsome—even late into his seventies and early eighties.

Rarely did Avent Childress talk about his family of origin, which—in retrospect—was too bad, because he had some illustrious forebears. Notably, as I mentioned, his great aunt, Sarah Childress, had married James K. Polk, eleventh president of the United States. Sarah had also come from Murfreesboro, Tennessee, where the Childress clan resided, and lived almost to her 88th birthday, surviving her illustrious husband as the doyenne of Nashville for over 40 years. Another forebear was James Adair Lyon, a highly respected Presbyterian clergyman. He had been my grandfather's uncle on his mother's side, and in addition to being scholarly and devout, had very ambivalent views on slavery throughout the Civil War, making him almost an abolitionist, despite his Southern heritage.

I was one of the few grandchildren of Avent Childress to make personal contact with his extended family, especially when my travels later took me into the Deep South. On one occasion I met with John Tune, whose mother, Charlotte Childress Tune, daughter of Bomp's brother, lived there. John was an up-and-coming civic-minded lawyer in Nashville who had been mayor of the city. He was also a recent convert to the Roman Catholic Church. He and I talked "religion" during what I recall as a very pleasant evening meeting. Shortly afterward, the cancer he had been struggling with got the better of him and he died. The John C. Tune (General Aviation) Airport in West Nashville was named for him.

I grew to love my grandfather, and even for a short period of time lived on the third floor of his and my grandmother's home at 8 Brayton Road in Scarsdale—a garret "apartment" used as digs by various family members over the decades, as needed. He lived only a short time beyond his wife, dying of bone cancer in the Greenwich, Connecticut, Hospital. His attending physician was his son-in-law, Dr. Gray Carter, then Physician-in-Chief. Gray Carter was married to Nana and Bomp's eldest daughter, Ann.

MADELEINE MACKAY CHILDRESS

Ah yes, Nana, as she was known to us all—at least by her nine grandchildren and many great-grandchildren that is. Socialite in her youth, as she loved to remind us, she made certain that those of us who would listen knew of her Gay Nineties upbringing, and of the various members of her family whose colorful pasts could have provided John Galsworthy with some fine character sketches for a great novel.

Her mother was a Barnes, daughter of Alfred S. Barnes, who established a publishing company that became the largest textbook publisher in the United States. Her father, George D. Mackay, was a successful entrepreneur in New York City, and for much of his adult life a devout Presbyterian. In his spare time he would give lectures on the life of Christ using stereopticon pictures of the paintings of Great Masters to illustrate his themes. He would call for commitments to Christ, and had some notable conversions—including a prostitute who later shared a bedroom with my grandmother at their Brooklyn townhouse.

George Mackay, as Nana told the story, had a dramatic conversion to Roman Catholicism on his return from a trip to the Holy Land with the evangelist Dwight L. Moody, who was a close personal friend. He and Moody had taken their families to Paris via ocean liner, then, leaving their families there, they traveled by train to Marseilles and by boat to Haifa. They followed this up with a donkey trip through the Holy Land. Together, my great- grandfather and Moody, who in addition to his evangelistic crusades founded Massachusetts' Northfield and Mt. Hermon Schools and the Moody Bible Institute of Chicago, retraced the steps of Jesus. On the return trip, Moody had chosen a separate itinerary. George Mackay met a Greek Orthodox priest on a ship on the Mediterranean and was deeply impressed by him. Their conversation revolved around the many divisions in Christendom and the search for the "perfect church." Much to Moody's dismay, I was told, my great grandfather converted to Roman Catholicism, bringing his whole family with him—with the exception of my grandmother, his eldest daughter. Madeline stood firmly on her previous Protestant and Evangelical understanding of the Bible, and despite a year at the Convent of the Sacred Heart on Manhattan's 91st Street, retained her strong biblical faith. In any event, the year at that strict Catholic School was a punishment for disobeying her parents by opening the Brooklyn townhouse in their absence to throw a party for her friends.

Madeline Mackay Childress must have cut quite a figure in Scarsdale, New York, in those days. With her four attractive, very sporty, sophisticated daughters who married well and all lived within 15 miles of her, she presided over an extended family that drew admiration and doubtless envy from some. Nana was a raconteur with a ready laugh, even when—as was often the case—she was the unwitting foil to her own story. Stylishly plump, wearing a print dress and a large straw hat, she could be seen at the American Yacht Club of a Sunday afternoon watching one daughter or another demolish the opposition on the tennis court, and then taking the waters in Long Island Sound. That was before those waters became so hopelessly polluted that the historic Club was forced to add a swimming pool.

BIBLE STORIES AND SUNDAY SCHOOL LESSONS

My own recollections of Nana go back to childhood when either Eric or I fell sick, and stayed home from school. She would appear and sit by our bedside, telling or reading us stories from the Bible. There was something about the way she told these stories that struck a responsive cord. She really believed the stories. She shared with us not only the well-known Old Testament sagas that she loved, but the New Testament stories as well. She also shared them with her highly attentive Sunday School class at St. James the Less where most of our extended family were members.

Madeline Childress had been nurtured by a number of famous Bible teachers of the day, most especially Donald Grey Barnhouse. He was a scholarly Presbyterian preacher from Philadelphia whose "empire" included a regular radio broadcast and a popular magazine *Eternity*. She loved her *Schofield Reference Bible,* whose notes taught her to be a strict dispensationalist, ever watchful for the immanent Second Coming of Christ. She was a teetotaler, and therefore no alcohol was ever served in the house, though rumors abounded about Bomp's imbibing a beer or an occasional mixed drink with his buddies at work or at the Club.

Nana's love of telling Sunday School students about the Second Coming, and their wide-eyed wonder at discovering this rarely taught classical Christian doctrine, got her into trouble with The Rev. Harry Price, rector of St. James the Less. Upon hearing a complaint from one parent, whose daughter, Marshall Braxton, returned home one Sunday with the exciting news that Jesus was coming back to earth, The Rev. Price decided that he had had enough. A liberal to the heart, he gently, though firmly, told my grandmother that she should cease and desist talking about the Second Coming to her students. That proved to be the last straw for Nana (and, as it turned out, for most of the rest of the family). At her suggestion we all promptly betook ourselves to a variety of churches, ending up just down the road from St. James at the newly-formed Trinity Lutheran Church (Missouri Synod). There we discovered an orthodoxy that was taught with a very firm hand. She and Bomp remained members there until their deaths. It always surprised me that she was permitted to take Holy Communion at Trinity despite the fact that, to the best of my knowledge, she was not a member. This was a sign to me that the Rev.

Brustadt, their pastor, must have bowed to social pressure, because it was against denominational policy to let any but committed LCMS members receive the sacrament. Bomp took Holy Communion just once in my memory, in the hospital after Nana had died. It must have been a great comfort to him and to Dr. Brustadt to share in the Lord's Supper together.

Two of my mother's sisters, Madeline Beck and Sally Auxford, returned to St. James the Less after brief stints as Lutherans, and remained there as loyal members until their deaths. I was privileged to give the homily at my aunt Sally's funeral (my other cousins and I always called by her first name, Sally, at her insistence). On that occasion the then acting rector made a point of telling the congregation of old Scarsdalians that the Episcopal Church "really did believe in the Second Coming of Christ." In short, the reason that the Childress clan originally left St. James had become part of the lore of that parish.

ALWAYS A RACONTEUR

Nana loved telling stories of her family, and had albums of photographs with which to feed the imagination. She had grown up a child of privilege in New York City's gilded age. There were balls and parties, and summers at fashionable Watch Hill, Rhode Island. In their heyday, her parents had left their Brooklyn townhouse and later an estate overlooking the Hudson in Yonkers, and migrated to the spacious hilltop farm in Chappaqua that I have mentioned. There her father built a large home surrounded by a wide veranda and a series of houses for his children. His three sons were each given apartments over the stables. For his first daughter, Madeline and her charming husband Avent, he built a lovely columned house that, as I mentioned, still stands. For his younger daughter, Lois and her husband Roland Elliman, cousin of the well-known New York realtor, he built a cottage with crisscross windows nicknamed Hookeynook. That cottage remains as the golf house for the Whippoorwill Country Club.

After Donald Mackay's conversion to Roman Catholicism, he provided summer quarters in Chappaqua for a variety of nuns and monks who would retreat there from the City's heat for rest and renewal. On one occasion, a woman calling herself the Abbess arrived with her nephew and managed to linger for virtually the whole summer. Nana loved to tell us about the Abbess, who would sit on the veranda in a rocking chair, and announce with a jocular voice to curious family members: "If you only knew who I really was…" Duped by her charisma, the family kept her on as a privileged guest. Later, after her departure, it became known that she was wanted in several states for grand larceny and her "nephew" was really a paramour!

But it was not for her colorful family stories that I remember Nana best. She introduced me to the Bible, and especially to an unabashed faith in Jesus Christ. The first inkling that I had of a personal relationship with God was in her dressing room where, when I was eight or nine, she read me portions of a little nineteenth century classic, *Intra Muros* by Rebecca Ruter Springer, still in print. It gives an allegorical picture of heaven, with images drawn from the Book of Revelation. We both cried at the wonder of what was to come. It was her lack of fear at the prospect of death and her eagerness to experience heaven that made me think that biblical faith might be true.

FAMILY RELATIONS

Growing up in a large extended family, all of whom lived fairly close to one another, gave me the advantage of knowing who I was at a young age. We were not immune to the usual family squabbles, and of course those uncles, aunts, and cousins who stood out in one way or another (for their wealth, personal quirks, achievements, or shameful antics) became stock-in-trade stories around our dinner table—either out of envy or sometimes a misplaced sense of personal superiority. But my recollections of Thanksgiving and Christmas dinners at Nana and Bomp's, with some 15 -20 family members gathered around the well-stocked tables all vying with each other to get a word in edgewise, provided a foundation of self-awareness that has lasted with me all my life. As I write this my parents' generation has all passed away, and now it is just cousins (and of course their children and children's children) who remain. Nevertheless, it is a treasure to look back at family photographs and let my fertile imagination bring back these events. With appreciative nostalgia, I can almost hear the laughter surrounding them.

Because Nana provided my first encounter with biblical faith, and because I loved her dearly, I find it hard to look back on her with an objective eye. I can now see defects in her character that totally escaped my notice as a child. But none of that dims my appreciation and affection. Appearances may have played too strong a role in her life. She tried to walk a tightrope between being "in" the world but not "of" it. And doubtless she fell off the rope one way or the other. With her inbred sense of privilege and strong character, she may have exercised too much control over those close to her, including her husband, who most of the time seemed reluctant to walk hand-in-hand with her faith. As I mentioned, he was only willing to profess that faith sacramentally after her death. But, as is true with us all, it is grace through faith that "justifies." It's not our behavior. And certainly it was faith that shone brightly in Madeleine Childress, a faith that was grounded on God's Word that pointed her to the risen Christ.

One notable exception to my grandfather's apparent religious reservations occurred when Billy Graham held his famous 1957 Madison Square Garden 16-week Crusade in New York City. It was a particular joy to me when both Nana and Bomp chartered a bus and filled it on several occasions with their Scarsdale friends and motored in to the Garden. It was on that occasion that Bomp's quiet faith, submerged under years of Wall Street cronyism and his wife's overt spirituality, were revealed with flying colors. I was proud of them both.

Two memories of my grandparents are worth recounting. In the mid- 1960's, Bomp was finally forced to empty his desk at Moore & Schley, the investment firm on Wall Street that he had faithfully served for decades. He needed a driver to take him into the City, and I offered. He was a very sad man who had finally come to the end of his career. There would be no more lunches with "the guys," no more deals over the phone, no more feelings of being needed. I ached for him as I read the emotions on his face, and watched as his former partners bid him goodbye. I saw his human side as never before.

My last vivid memory of my grandmother typically involved humor. Gathered around the dining room table were an assortment of aunts, uncles, and cousins, plus my mother and me. Nana, who was showing definite signs of creeping dementia, regaled us with her usual stories. Each one began with its own unique introduction, but as the stories unfolded, each one turned out to be the very same story. Then, she turned to my mother across the table, looked at her and then looked over at me, and then back to my mother. She must have thought I was my father, because with a clear voice she asked: "Now tell us, when did you two first meet?" I was allowed the privilege of speaking at her funeral held at Trinity Lutheran Church in Scarsdale, the place where she and Bomp had worshiped for so many years.

MARY-ADAIR CHILDRESS MOORE

I have purposefully left my mother until now because she was doubtless the strongest influence on me. She was also the one family member with whom I had the most conflict—which is not surprising for a son eager to emerge from under parental control.

Mary Adair Childress, her maiden name, was the third daughter of Avent and Madeline Childress. I learned relatively little of her childhood other than the fact that she grew up with a sense of inferiority. She thought herself less loved by her parents than her two older sisters Ann and Madeline were, and also less loved than the "baby" of the family, her younger sister Sally. She showed signs of mild delinquency as a child, painting some white walls in a new house under construction in the neighborhood black. But being a third daughter gave her a strong competitive streak. She was not especially academic, although she did graduate from the Spence School in Manhattan, commuting by rail from Scarsdale each day. Where she did excel was in tennis. As a singles player she was truly excellent, and as I grew up I noticed our dining room sideboard gradually fill with a great assortment of silver trophies that she had won in this tournament or that.

Mom had little time for religion—although it should be said that she and all three of her sisters eventually developed an apparently orthodox Christian faith. In her younger days however, like her sisters, my mother was too busy attending parties, living what was then called "the gay life," and trying to find herself. Her marriage to my father seems to have happened without a great deal of wisdom evident—or even romance. There was a "matter of factness" about their relationship that was later blamed alternately on his lack of demonstrative affection or her competitive nature. They entered the Scarsdale social scene, moving in and out of a set of couples who were mostly much better off than they were.

Mom excelled at cocktail parties. She dressed exceptionally well and was strikingly pretty (though not quite as glamorous as the touched up Hal Fyfe photographic portrait of her, taken in her early forties). She also drank heavily, and smoked up a storm. Her advice to my brother Eric and me, when we came along, consisted of moralistic one-liners, memorable though hardly profound: "Handsome is as handsome does;" "If at first you don't succeed, try, try again", "A bird in the hand is worth two in the bush", and so on. Clearly, she was a lost soul, hiding that fact behind a façade of superficial bonhomie.

She loved Eric and me equally, at least until later in life when she and Eric developed a special bond that lasted until her death. I shall get to that period eventually. But I grew up in a home that I thought was normal, loving, "cool" (though we would not have used that word then), and bright. I remember with particular joy her reading us *The Swiss Family Robinson* when we were young. What we lacked in an appreciation of high culture—neither great literature nor classical music being subjects of much interest in our home—we made up for in sports and family fun. Picnics with other families, walks on Sunday afternoon, card games by the fire in winter, and cozy suppers of creamed chip beef on toast were standard fare.

As I mentioned earlier, Mom, or Maizie as she preferred to be called, had little time for church. Eric and I were dropped off at Sunday School, after which we walked the short distance from St.

James the Less to the Fox Meadow Tennis Club, to meet our parents for lunch and an afternoon of tennis. Later, in our teen years, we would meet at the more upscale Manursing Island Club in Rye. But that early pattern clearly communicated to us the idea that religion is an important part of life, good like nutrition, but not to become a central focus.

CHAPTER 3

SUBURBAN MEMORIES

THE MAIZIE SHOP

Money was always an issue as we grew up in the affluent suburb some twenty-two miles due north of the City. Dad had survived the Great Depression as a very young man, and had escaped overseas military service during World War II because of his size, but he was making barely enough to support us all. So Mom tried a variety of schemes to supplement his income. Once she tried selling oranges imported from Florida to friends and neighbors, but the idea collapsed when they arrived frozen. Then she hit on a less risky and more promising idea: Scarsdale was filled with well-heeled women, many on clothes' allowances from their husbands. So there had to be closets full of dresses and such that these women might sell for cash or swap for updated outfits.

The business began in my bedroom one day when I was about 8 years old. Some of Mom's wealthy friends from Greenwich came down and put their own clothes up on consignment. Thus the Maizie Shop was born.

Taking 25% of the ticket price as her commission, and offering the nearly-new and typically elegant clothes at a reasonable price, she soon found herself operating a thriving little business. In a couple of years, the shop moved to a store in nearby Hartsdale, and has recently celebrated its 70th year. Although such consignment shops are found all over the country today, hers was one of the first of its kind, if not *the* first. Her attention to quality as well as her business acumen kept the shop going, and growing. She worked tirelessly, but she always took care to look elegant herself, and with her earnings she managed to put both Eric and me through boarding school.

Mom also purchased a summer home in Old Black Point, a tony enclave on the Connecticut shore near New London. Each August we would leave New York suburbia behind and, with a maid in tow, head for Black Point where there would be lots of tennis, an active beach life, croquet (there pronounced "krokey", not "krokay", please!), and non-stop cocktail parties. Eric and I were assigned major chores each day, to keep us from the degenerate life of the youth of the community. This meant cutting the endless hedges around the house, or—one summer—painting the house itself. Like Tom Sawyer, we managed to gather most of the other teen-agers from the small community around us while we painted, and soon we were at the center of a social set that was accustomed to considerably more wealth and leisure than we.

NEW YORK SOCIETY

Through this social set, we were introduced to New York society. There were cotillions, balls, coming out parties, and dinners on Park and Fifth Avenues to which we were invited as escorts dressed in tuxedos or, even sometimes, white tie and tails. On one occasion, I was the escort of Ellen Berlin, daughter of songwriter Irving Berlin. The evening began at the Berlins' Beekman Place townhouse and moved on to The Pierre Hotel until "breakfast" was fashionably served at midnight. Dancing with Ellen, I committed the ultimate *faux pas* of asking whether the emerald and diamond necklace, earrings, and bracelet she was wearing were real. "Yes", Ellen said, "they are." "Where did you get them?" I asked, digging a deeper hole in the ground with each ridiculous question. "Daddy gave them to me." "Oh, when was that?" She replied nonchalantly, "When I was born."

Soon I learned how to comport myself in the heady world of high society, chatting amiably with band leaders like Meyer Levin and Ben Cutler (who had once dated our mother). I was entertained at elegant New York City homes like that of the Lawrence Rockefellers and treated to dinner at swank restaurants like Twenty-One. The high water mark of my foray into this extraordinary culture was the coming out party of Laura Rockefeller in the Rainbow Room high atop Rockefeller Center. There, along with three hundred or so other young guests, I was treated to Chateaubriand, baked Alaska flambé, and a private performance of the celebrated dancers known as the Rockettes—a mere ten feet away. When Lawrence Rockefeller rose to toast his daughter, he told us that he hoped we'd all be back for his next daughter's coming out party. I made a mental note to put it on my calendar!

A BUDDING KLEPTOMANIAC

But I am, of course, way ahead of myself. My childhood was not altogether pleasant, nor was I, by all accounts, any candidate for sainthood. My religious convictions and my moral behavior were not moving forward on a parallel track. My grandmother had instilled in me a strong Protestant view of the Bible and, when I was nine years old, this led to intense debates on the Pope and the Virgin Mary with Clare Henry, the Catholic girl who lived across the street.

At the same time I was something of a kleptomaniac. Hidden underneath some lingerie in my mother's bottom drawer was "the gambling bank." It was an old evening purse that held the winnings from my parents' card games with other couples. The "bank" was a veritable treasure trove of coins and small bills, to which I began helping myself with increasing frequency. This supply of cash supplemented my small allowance, and together with the earnings from various little chores for neighbors, gave me enough money to purchase a drawer full of toys and later candy exceeding my wildest dreams. Why my parents never really figured out the trick, I do not know.

My kleptomaniacal tendencies did come home to roost, however, when I was in first grade. I was in love—puppy love—with a young damsel named Nancy Moore. We would conspire about how, when we were married, she would not have to change her name! One Christmas, Mrs. Moore (Nancy's mother) called my mother. "Do you know what Peter gave to Nancy?" she asked. My mother, of course, didn't know. "Well, on a tiny satin pillow in a little box that must have once held a perfume bottle, Peter had arranged a neatly folded, crisp ten dollar bill." Of course I had stolen the bill from the cache I mentioned earlier, and, when I admitted that, was firmly but gently reprimanded. Sadly, this did not put an end to my habit of stealing, but it definitely put a dent in it.

Many of my childhood friendships were ones in which I felt I had the upper hand. As I was more sensitive than other boys, I tended to choose unthreatening companions whom I could easily influence. Only one of these friendships has survived into adulthood, a testimony more to his loyalty than mine, I'm ashamed to say. My artistic and sensitive nature caused me to cultivate a creative side that I thought would blossom into a full-blown career. I drew and painted. I took piano lessons, but discovered that regular practice was not for me, though I retained the ability to play about six songs from memory well into my adult years—fooling many that I actually knew how to play the piano. Because I also loved architecture, a love nurtured by the ongoing construction of houses in a wide variety of architectural styles in my home town over the years, I told myself that I wanted to be an architect when I grew up. That ambition lasted until my father explained that I not only had to make houses look nice, I also had to make them stand up. With utterly no interest in the engineering side of the matter, I eventually gave up my vision. But my interest in the history of architecture was later aroused at Yale by two courses I took from the renowned Vincent Scully. Music, art, and especially architecture remain fascinations of mine to this day.

WORLD WAR II

Living through World War II in my grade school years left me with a number of vivid memories. There was the "Victory" vegetable garden that replaced the grassy play area in our back yard. There were black shades that had to be drawn at night, especially when the air raid siren went off. Dad had to patrol the neighborhood to make sure that no lights could be seen from the sky. There was the large picnic in upper Westchester when all the fathers quietly and suddenly disappeared into the woods because one of them thought he spotted a parachute on the ground. A German dropped behind enemy lines? There was food rationing, making the time when I found a priceless book of meat rations on the sidewalk in nearby White Plains feel like a bonanza. Especially intriguing was the discovery, a couple of miles up the road from our house, of two German émigrés with a basement full of electronic equipment. They had apparently been sending secret messages to Europe.

My most vivid wartime memory centered on the time when a friend, Bobby Medley, and I went off on a hike and picnic to the Scarsdale Golf Club course. Our route took us down Fenimore Road and through the village of Hartsdale. There, walking along an unpaved delivery area behind some stores, kicking tin cans and empty boxes as we walked, I laid into a large solid cardboard sphere. It turned out to be a drum full of Lewis Sherry French Vanilla ice cream—15 pounds of the glorious stuff. The thought that it was our responsibility to find the store from whose delivery truck this treasure had fallen to the ground never occurred to us. "Finders keepers . . ." was our motto. So, because it was a very hot day, we carefully laid the container in a nearby brook to keep it from melting, and later hauled it back to Bobby's house, which was closer to the village than mine. I filled several containers with ice cream and took them home, leaving the rest in his freezer until I could come back the next day and collect the rest of my share. But this was a time of serious food rationing and, unfortunately for me, Bobby's sister held a slumber party that night, and all the remaining ice cream was consumed. I wrote about the incident in a letter to my Aunt Peggy in Texas, and she in turn forwarded it on to her husband, Ed Petersen, who was stationed on a South Pacific island. He reportedly gathered a group of his buddies around and said: "You've got to hear this story…"

What with my stories of secret stashes of candy and treasured finds of ice cream, you are probably guessing that food had become rather more important to me than it should have. Sweets particularly. This fascination showed not only in the growing number of cavities in my teeth, but more noticeably in the size of my stomach. So for several years from, say, 10-14, I was in danger of becoming what my mother disparagingly called a “pasty-faced fat boy.” Nor was I as manly as my Dad wished. On one occasion, he purchased a punching bag for my birthday. It remained mostly unused in the attic. More important, he urged Eric and me to play football. Dad had been a football player at prep school and at Yale, and so it was natural for him to expect us to follow in his footsteps. We began when I was in grade school with what amounted to a “little league.” Many a family laugh was had at my expense as Mom, Dad and Eric imagined me, a wary linesman, accidentally receiving a pass and running not towards the other team’s goal, but in the opposite direction—so that I would not get hurt by being tackled.

But the most painful memory of these awkward childhood days was the night, when I was very young, when all three other members of the family held me down on the carpet, laughing, and a face was painted on my stomach with Iodine. I was squeamish about pain, and thus I hated the stinging antiseptic Iodine. The experience was intended to teach me that it was not an enemy and that I should not cry when Iodine was applied. Decades later, at Dad’s eightieth birthday party, I recalled to the assembled crowd that shaming and humiliating incident, and publicly forgave him with a smile. And, yes, he remembered the occasion just as vividly as I.

Growing up in World War II suburbia without a lot of discretionary money to go around meant summer jobs, weekend jobs, and chores around the house. As I grew older, I assisted a lady who distributed books from her own private lending library. I gardened for pennies on the dollar, simonized neighbor’s cars, pet sat their animals, cleaned houses, clipped their hedges, and even worked in the US Post Office one Christmas. As a family, we were conscious of money, and our lack of it, from a very early age. Only after my great uncle, Edwin Bayles, died and left my father with a tidy supplementary income did our family fortunes turn the corner. Bigger, fancier cars were bought, the house was decorated, and we acquired that summer home in Old Black Point.

JARRETT, VIRGINIA

In those early post-World War II years, families didn't travel as much or as far as they did later. Only the very wealthy could afford ski vacations, cruises to the Caribbean, or summers spent at dude ranches out West.

Our first family trip was typical of the era. Eager to show Eric and me something other than the greater New York City area, which, was not after all the center of the world, Mom and Dad decided on a family trip to Washington and Virginia. I think the year was 1947, just two years after the war had ended. Because we would be visiting a Johns Manville plant in Jarrett, Virginia, Dad could write it off as a business expense.

Journeys in those days were long and arduous. The Interstate system had not yet been built, so there was no I-95. We made our way down Route 1, stopping at endless traffic lights and smelling the foul New Jersey "flats" where oil refineries spewed noxious fumes. Finally, on our first night, we arrived at Baltimore. I recall being kept awake that first night by the neon signage of our hotel, flashing just outside our window, and hearing the start-up engines of an endless stream of 24-wheeler trucks at the traffic lights just below.

But we made it to Washington. There my sense of patriotism grew exponentially as we toured the Lincoln and Washington Memorials, gazed at the White House and the Capitol, and explored Arlington

Cemetery. But it was Williamsburg that really caught my attention, on account of my love of architecture. It gave me a glimpse of what colonial America looked like, and I relished a newfound sense of our national history.

One night we entered the elegant Williamsburg Inn for dinner. After we were seated and had already begun drinking water from our glasses, Dad gazed at the prices on the menu. Gently and with some dignity, he whispered to us that we would not be staying for dinner. Rather than being embarrassed and humiliated, I recall being proud of him for his willingness to economize when needed.

A truly entertaining leg of the trip included a drive along the Skyline Drive through the Blue Ridge. This remarkable parkway was built during the Depression as a Public Works project. We picnicked along the sides of quiet country roads. Unfortunately, after one picnic, Mom found that a glass bottle of milk had gone sour and tossed it out of the back window of the car. The only problem was that the window was not open. The stench of that sour milk stayed with us for a very long time.

But our most amusing memory of this first big family trip was Jarrett, Virginia. Jarrett was a sleepy backwater where Johns Manville, a leading manufacturer of building materials, insulation, and roofing, had a plant. We holed up in Sykes hotel, the only one in town, while Dad made his obligatory tour. That night we found ourselves all bedded together in one large dormitory with cockroaches climbing the wall. Dinner consisted of "chicken stewed in its own juice," a distinctly unappetizing item that was the sole offering on the menu. At breakfast the next morning, someone else's jam was still in the butter we found on our table. We laughed as a family for years about the commercial hospitality available in Jarrett in those days, and especially about the details of our overnight stay at Sykes Hotel.

GAINING A WORK ETHIC

In addition to chores around the house, which included washing dishes each evening, emptying garbage cans, wiping fingerprints off woodwork, sweeping the basement and garage, clipping hedges and mowing the lawn, we were expected to contribute towards our own allowances by securing jobs in the neighborhood.

In winter, there was always snow shoveling. In summer, there were neighbors' gardens to care for and cars to wash and wax. No job was too menial, despite meager pay. In those days, a dollar was considered real money.

After work, play eventually happened. Much of our play involved local and regional tennis tournaments for "boys" (those 15 and under) and later "juniors" (those 15-18). Often these tournaments were combined with social events at the homes of parents, and in the case of the Manursing Island Club of Rye, New York, with a gala "tennis week" for teams from a wide variety of prep schools. After a day's competition on the courts, each evening there would be a huge dinner dance at one of the town's many clubs. One had a sense that Rye's matrons were seriously eyeing future escorts for their daughters from among the teen-aged athletes dancing in their Madras or white dinner jackets.

Eric and I even managed to win an Eastern tennis ranking: #1 boys doubles in the East. We lost in the finals to two brothers from Ft. Lauderdale, but as Florida was not technically "East" in the eyes of the U.S. Lawn Tennis Association, we emerged with a ranking. Our win was largely due to Eric's prowess. His left-handed serve was nearly always lethal, and his net game far better than my own. But my forehand was at least a minor asset.

FAMILY LIFE

I had a decidedly inventive streak. You may have noticed that adults tend to remember the extremes of weather during their childhoods. Whether global warming, the current political orthodoxy, is a fact or a fantasy is still to be decided. But childhood memories often recollect great storms, heat waves, and blizzards. I grew up with stories of the "Blizzard of 88." That Nor'easter began on March 11, 1888, and continued for three days, dropping 50 inches of snow in Connecticut and New Jersey, and 40 inches on New York City. We had nothing like that to brag about, although there were tornadoes, floods, and heavy snows that did leave piles of the wonderful white stuff to play in. I recall one where when I was about eight. I built a snow house on the edge of our yard. It had a wooden ceiling, and snow covered the whole thing like an igloo. With a watering can I sprayed water on top so that after a very cold night the entire building became almost rock solid. Inside I placed an old rug, furniture, and various other domestic appurtenances. One of my early life's great disappointments was the day when a huge snowplow managed to cart the whole thing away in one fell swoop.

Back now to my mother, that inveterate competitor, hard-working businesswoman, and loving parent. With an almost total lack of discipline in her social life (later I learned that she had had a brief affair while married to my father, and he doubtless had had one or two while married to her), she began drinking heavily. There was no tradition of alcoholism in either family, though both my parents were slowly gravitating from social drinkers into something close to alcoholism. When I was around eight years old, I recall Mom coming home from a party and slipping into Eric's and my bedroom to give us a hug and say goodnight. There was more than a whiff of alcohol on her breath, and she was woozy, if not drunk. I remember sitting bolt upright in bed, and surprising myself—and no doubt her—by firmly insisting: "Mom, I don't ever want to see you this way again."

Some arguments between my parents were unpleasant to overhear. Often they occurred while Dad was bookkeeping for The Maizie Shop. Mom's entrepreneurial skills did not extend to careful record keeping, and Dad's perfectionism was frequently stretched to the limits. "Maizie, what did Mrs. Hellman pay for the yellow silk shantung sheath?" he would shout from his living room desk to somewhere else in the house. My brother and I would write off these outbursts to a hard day at the office, because Dad had an oppressive and emasculating boss for most of his working life. But they clearly revealed some unhealthy trends in our parents' marriage—trends that were later to erupt into serious conflict and ultimately divorce.

Both parents could be stern disciplinarians on occasion. During most summer days, Eric and I would arrive at the breakfast table to find a list of chores written out on a large yellow pad. They had to be completed before we enjoyed any play. One of my typical chores was going through the house with Old Dutch Cleanser and a damp cloth, removing all our fingerprints from woodwork and walls. This duty nourished a mildly compulsive aspect of my personality, such that throughout my life clean cars, woodwork, clothes, and floors became something of a quiet obsession. Both Mom and Dad would resort to corporal punishment when needed. I accepted this as normal, and recall a number of firm spankings that really hurt. Mom, on one occasion, was particularly frustrated with Eric and when he was quite young sent him into the field next door to our house to pick a switch so that she could give him a whipping. He cleverly came back with a leafy bough that he knew would be far less painful than a smooth single stalk.

As a mother, Mom was quick with advice, but not particularly gifted at listening. She was far too much a do-er and an activist to listen. However, she had a deeply empathic side, and when she spotted either Eric or me hurting, she could be very understanding. During one of our earliest summers at Old Black Point she realized that, as a young teen-ager, I had not yet been accepted by the social set of my peers, and was quite lonely. I would take long bike rides to a store where I could buy candy, and I must have unburdened myself to her in unmistakable ways. She went out of her way that summer to play cards with me, and to help me accept my situation. I recall endless games of Canasta! The next summer I was accepted, and no longer needed her comfort in the same way.

SPIRITUAL QUEST

Beneath all the activity, competition, busyness and partying there was clearly a very deep hole in Mom's inner being. I would describe her nature as more "soulish" than spiritual. She was clearly searching for something to fill the vacuum that a souring marriage and a town full of fair-weather friends could not fill. Her search coincided with Eric going off to boarding school at the age of 15, and my preparing to do so a year later. As the empty nest loomed on the horizon, and as there was little emotional support from Dad, Mom was crying out for help. But where could she turn?

One natural source of comfort and guidance would have been her mother. After all, Nana lived just a mile away, professed a vigorous Christian faith, and presumably knew her daughter well enough to point her in the right direction. Perhaps Mom tried that avenue; but she soon found that the advice given was inadequate to her needs. With what soon emerged as a near fanatic religious devotion, Mom began to question her mother's spiritual integrity. This led to years of sad and painful separation in the family. I shall return to that later in my story.

Despite that, Mom's spiritual quest was genuine. Few people of her background in those days, at least in our circle of friends, professed to have had an encounter with God. It was simply not "on" to talk about these things, and in that heyday of Protestant liberalism, few if any of the suburban churches in our town knew about small group Bible study, prayer groups, or other venues where one could really experience God in a personal way. Evangelism was a dirty word in mainline Protestantism, even though Billy Graham's crusades were taking off and some church people, though certainly not the liberal clergy, were coming to accept the validity of his unique ministry. However, among the country club group, the cocktail party set of which my parents were a part, very few—if any—knew (or would admit to knowing) what a personal relationship with Christ was all about. Nana did, of course, but immersion in the mainstream social environment of the day precluded her from knowing where to direct her searching daughter.

Mom found her answer in the Bible and at the local branch of the Christian and Missionary Alliance Church—a church to which maids and house servants might have gone, but in which ladies and gentlemen of my parents' ilk would not be seen dead. She soaked up everything that she heard, and was there every time the doors were open. My brother and I also went although, despite our own spiritual rumblings, the C & M A was worlds away from the life we had come to know.

Unfortunately, Mom sought out and was taken under the wing of an older mentor, Nettie Longyear. Nettie was a domineering elder lady with very decisive views on sanctification. Under her tutelage,

Mom was taught that she should "come out from among them and be separate" (2 Cor. 6:17), a verse that Nettie interpreted to mean that Christians should have nothing to do with their former "worldly" friends, unless they expressed an interest in the faith.

This led to a major crisis in the family as Mom pulled away from all social interaction with those who did not show an interest in a deep and overt Christian faith. She would not even play sports with them.

Naturally, Dad was disturbed, and deeply so. For one thing, he and Mom were no longer intimate. For another, the social set in which they moved had begun to think his wife had gone crazy. On one occasion after our parents had separated, Hi Tarnower, better known as Dr. Herman Tarnower, paid the house an unscheduled visit. He had been on the fringe of my parents' social set, and was our family doctor as well. He dropped in ostensibly to pay a personal call but it was painfully obvious, as I watched and listened from a distance, that he was there to check on Mom's sanity. Almost certainly he had been put up to the visit by some member of the wider family. (Dr. Tarnower later became famous as the "Scarsdale Diet Doctor" who was murdered by Jean Harris, the headmistress of Madeira School, with whom he had had a notorious affair.)

Things began to unravel between our parents while Eric and I were away at college. As I returned home from New Haven at the end of my freshman year in June of 1955, Dad announced to us in a painful private meeting that he was going to get a formal separation from Mom and would be moving out of the house. Even though we were not surprised, we were deeply saddened. After all, in our ignorance we thought we had been the "perfect family" up until that time. Dad did move out, and ultimately spent a summer in

Reno, Nevada, securing a divorce on the grounds of "extreme mental cruelty."

TURBULENT TEENS

Where had I been when all this was happening? At fourteen, I had chosen to follow my brother (and father's) footsteps and go off to boarding school. I was at St. Mark's, a respected Episcopal Church boarding school in Southborough, Massachusetts. My Scarsdale High School classmates seemed confused at this choice, ours being considered one of the finest public high schools in the country. But as my life unfolded in later years, I could see the hand of God guiding this decision in unmistakable ways.

At St. Mark's, as at Old Black Point, I was introduced to a culture that was dominated by people with considerable wealth. By no means were all the boys from wealthy backgrounds. There were boys like my brother and me whose families had more modest means. But the underlying assumptions of the School had been subtly crafted by moneyed people. Nothing made this more evident to me than a line from Louis Auchincloss's *The Rector of Justin*, the novelized story of the Rev. Endicott Peabody, the founding headmaster of Groton School. The line goes something like this: "He may have thought that he was raising up soldiers for the Church; but what he was really doing was teaching mammon the comportment of a gentleman." This was, of course, well disguised at St. Mark's, where boys were consigned to live in sparse cubicles in large dormitories separated from one another only by a flimsy curtain, where ruggedness on the sports field was highly prized, and where a typical Sunday afternoon recreation might include tea with a master and his wife in a simple faculty home. Wealth came out, however, during vacations when boys would be spirited off to exotic watering holes like Palm Beach for Spring Break, or during term time when on a parents' weekend a couple of South American parents might appear in a sleek Rolls Royce to visit their son.

I was befriended by Peter Carleton, who quickly became my roommate, and for several years my best friend. Thanks to him, I was invited to spend spring vacation in Palm Beach with his grandparents, Mr. and Mrs. Harry Freylinguysen. They maintained estates there, and in Morristown, New Jersey, and also had a splendid pad on Park Avenue in New York City—not to mention a private railroad car in which they were escorted in grand style each season back and forth from New Jersey to Florida. In March of 1951, the Freyinghuysen's chauffeur Howles, met Peter and me at the West Palm Beach airport. For the next two weeks, I was flung into a world of extreme luxury and indulgence. Soon, a convertible, one of a mere five cars in the garage, was put at our disposal, and membership in every beach and golf Club in town was taken as a given. There were so many servants at the Frelinghuysen estate on El Bravo Way that there appeared to be a servant for the servants. I poked my head into the kitchen one day by accident, and saw a total stranger serving 10 or 12 servants at a formal dining table reserved for them.

But my own search for something deeper had only just begun, and despite the allure of all this magnificence (or perhaps because I could see that it was all very thin), I was in pursuit of God, barely knowing what I was looking for. As with all conversions, and I use that word in a classical Christian sense, rather than in a saw dust trail sense, many influences beared upon me. First, of course, my grandmother had introduced me to the Bible in a vivid, believable way. She continued to influence me at boarding school by sending the odd tract or sermon in the mail, and by ensuring that I had a

Bible in my suitcase when I left home. She had inscribed in my Bible: "Read it to be wise. Believe it to be safe. Practice it to be holy." I took her advice seriously.

ST MARK'S SCHOOL

But St. Mark's also had a strong influence on my spiritual quest. Each evening, students attended chapel. Each morning before classes began we said the Lord's Prayer together, with the headmaster leading us. Hymns, mostly the great hymns of the church, were sung by the boys, usually with gusto. Holy Communion was offered weekly on Wednesdays and then again on Sundays. This was a religious school, even though personal faith was rarely talked about. Yet for the life of me I couldn't find anyone to whom my own quest for a living faith made much sense. Anything to do with Billy Graham was anathema, even to the chaplains. Evangelism was ridiculed as mere emotionalism. Moreover, the chaplains, who were all bachelors, seemed to have even more questions about our faith than I. One of them couldn't believe in the Ascension of Christ, and had problems with miracles. A second wrote blood-curdling murder mysteries in his spare time. These were not men who inspired me as living examples of people who loved and followed Christ, whatever their private devotion may have been like.

But beyond all other influences, what really caught my attention was the Bible itself. Reading it at bedtime greatly calmed my spirit. My roommate was reading *MAD* comics and glaring at me from across the room, thinking that *I* was very strange. But in that Bible, my first one, I underlined passages that stood out, or that spoke to my need. As I read, I sensed the Holy Spirit coming through. The written Word fed my growing inner life, so that when I took long walks on a Sunday afternoon, or pondered the meaning of Christ while kneeling in chapel, I began to glimpse the Reality behind it all.

Doubtless, my struggles for acceptance among my peers were a factor. I had not been especially popular from the start, though I think I was credited with having some integrity. But being in the "in" crowd is extremely important in one's teens, and only a few manage to achieve that lofty status. Fortunately, being a good tennis player, and eventually captain of the team two years running, helped me. But I don't think I never quite achieved popularity.

However, our Old Black Point connections had catapulted my brother Eric and me into the heady world of New York City society anyway. Because we had the "right" pedigree, were at the "right" prep school, and were kind to the girls we dated, we were sought out as escorts. We escorted girls decked out in expensive gowns to little private dinner parties held at Upper East Side apartments and townhouses and then to elegant dances featuring well-known bands playing in upscale hotel ballrooms. Irving Berlin made a cameo appearance at a dinner party in his own home on one such occasion. At another event at Lawrence Rockefeller's triplex Fifth Avenue penthouse I remember seeing the portrait of Laura Spellman Rockefeller, in the dining room. Her eyes had been painted in such a way that they followed each person in the room wherever they went. Beneath the vast dining room table was a hidden console that allowed the head of the table to control a grand repertoire of music to complement each dinner course with the touch of a finger. This was probably as close to "royalty" as I ever got.

Despite these substantial social advantages, I ran afoul of my classmates at St. Marks in an incident that led to a crisis that altered my relationship with a number of them.

Cigarettes were absolutely forbidden at boarding school to all but seniors (Sixth Formers, as they were called). Also, certain places in town were "out of bounds." Nevertheless, as boys will do, a fairly large group of us intentionally strayed out of bounds one Sunday afternoon and started smoking. This was my second year at school, and my brother was a monitor—a member of the senior class's governing council. Of course, I had smoked the odd cigarette "behind the barn" so to speak. But this incident was a clear, public infringement of school rules, and I was frankly troubled by the attitude of the other boys who were in my class and the one above me.

Because of my sense that something was wrong, I was the only one that day who didn't smoke. My conscience troubled, I returned to campus and sought out my brother. "Who were the ones smoking?" Eric asked me. I thought the question was completely innocent. But with that high sense of duty often found in firstborns, he decided to hand the names over to the authorities. The boys were hauled before the august headmaster, Bill Barber, and while not expelled or suspended, they were given a stern warning. The headmaster followed up with a letter sent home to each parent. Naturally, it took very little time for those caught to figure out how the news had been leaked. Ultimately, several members of the class above me forgave me for what they came to accept as an innocent slip of the tongue. But many in my own class could not. Several years later, one classmate said to me: "Peter, I will never forgive you."

That and other shaming incidents clouded my St. Mark's career. But whoever said boarding school was supposed to be a happy experience? What I learned from those four years greatly out weighed the pain. I learned to get along with people I did not necessarily like, to express my views clearly, to write fairly well, to study hard, to compete in sports I didn't particularly enjoy, in short to find my own way in a normal social environment.

Plus, I was living at an influential elite boarding school and could see that without God in their lives, these young people were just as lost as I. Thankfully, I never fell into the trap of thinking that just because they were privileged in terms of money, education, travel, and so on, these boys didn't have as deep a void in their lives as I. That growing awareness of their lostness was to shape my life, as my story will tell.

TURNING POINT

Fortunately for me, my sense of shame morphed into a sense of guilt. "O happy guilt" as Augustine put it, certainly captured my experience. Guilt, as opposed to shame, signifies real (not imagined) infractions of God's law, and by the time I was sixteen I had enough real infractions on the debit side of my ledger to weigh me down. I was guilty of one of those infractions in late July at Black Point. I had arrived a few days before the houses that had been fixed up for renting were turned over to their new tenants, and at the suggestion of an older boy whom I was eager to impress, I had joined him in trashing one of those houses. We tore the place apart, overturning wastebaskets, throwing pillows all over the room, unmaking beds, and generally wreaking havoc. The new tenants arrived to discover a total mess.

Word got out in the small summer community that someone had done a terrible thing, and a few days later my conscience could no longer permit me to remain silent. I confessed to my parents who sent me to the "mayor" of the community, and eventually to the new tenants. I expressed my sorrow, offered my apologies, and then did manual work for them to compensate them for their loss. Incidents like these moved me from a shame-orientation to a guilt-orientation. So, when I encountered the Good News of God's forgiveness in the Bible, sang of it in school hymns, and listened to it on Billy Graham's radio broadcast, *The Hour of Decision*, my heart was ready.

In 1952 I experienced a major turning point around Easter. I was back at school after March break, and we were just entering Holy Week. I had many questions about Jesus Christ. I was drawn to him, but I didn't know where he fit into the whole scheme of Christian experience.

One evening, long after lights were out and we boys were all supposed to be in bed, I snuck out of my room, tiptoed down the hall, descended the tower stairway, and entered the dimly lit chapel. I sat in the headmaster's chair, and peered into the darkness. Only the candle above the altar was lit, and I felt very alone. I began to think about the Resurrection of Jesus. Growing up in the Episcopal Church, being confirmed, and saying the Creed Sunday after Sunday, I naturally believed in the Resurrection. But it had never dawned on me until that evening what it meant. It certainly did not mean that Jesus rose, appeared to various disciples, and then went off to the desert somewhere to die again. What it did mean was that he had been crucified, he had died, and then he had risen to a new and glorious life, never to die again. If that was so, I reasoned, then he must be still alive now. And, if alive, then it must be theoretically possible for people to communicate with him.

Hesitantly, I began to speak to Jesus, forming the words in my mind. And, to my surprise, I had the distinct feeling that I was no longer alone. Someone was listening, and responding to me. Yes, he was alive now, and yes I could have a relationship with him.

I wish I could say that tears of joy began to fall down my cheek, or that a rush of emotion filled my aching heart. None of that happened. But what did happen was that a quiet awareness of Christ's presence entered my consciousness, and a deep assurance that he was real began to fill my mind. Was this conversion? It was certainly part of one, and an important part of one at that. My heart had been captured, and my mind had found a resting place.

What remained unconverted, or at least not fully converted, was my will. Therein lay an ongoing struggle. It was initially resolved some time later, but I have since discovered that it needs to be re-resolved daily as I still try to take back what I first surrendered, the fruitless endeavor to be master of my own life.

Something else happened too, as a result of that encounter. I was given a boldness to confess Christ to my classmates and to others. "Something has happened to you, Peter," my roommate, Peter Carleton observed, noticing the change that had come over me. He had been telling everyone that he wanted to become an Episcopal priest and later lived to regret that early enthusiasm, because the seed of his nascent faith never grew into a living plant. I, on the other hand, kept very quiet about any professional aspirations toward the ordained ministry. That was wise because I still had some fundamental reservations about it being a proper path for me. But I did make Christ known in conversations, whenever asked.

I made my most public confession at St. Mark's in a six-minute speech as part of a public speaking contest when I was in the equivalent of Grade Twelve. I had won the public speaking prize in my fifth form (eleventh grade) year with a hypothetical talk about Paris—a place I had never visited. It was slightly humorous and completely fabricated. But I had fun with the topic, and people enjoyed the talk.

Now I was speaking as a sixth former (twelfth grader), and I chose to talk about Billy Graham. It was the spring of 1954 and he had just hit the headlines on account of his London Crusade at Harringay Arena. Queen Elizabeth had received Graham warmly, as had the Archbishop of Canterbury. Many Church of England clergy and bishops had played active parts in his historic crusade. Because our American Episcopal church had historic ties to the Church of England, I felt that our members should at least be aware that this evangelist was not just some hick Baptist charlatan from Appalachia. Sadly that was the impression of most at my school, including the chaplains. I do not know if any minds were changed by my talk, nor did I win the prize that year. But I did my best to convey the impression that Christianity was more than "churchianity," and that faith could be personal and vital to one's daily life. And I nailed my colors to the mast.

CHAPTER 4

THE 1950'S

CULTURE

As my story implies, I was bred into and shaped by a certain culture in the Northeastern United States. "Middle class?" "Upper middle class?" Which was it? Certainly our connections put us in the latter category. However, for most of my growing years our family finances put us in the former. As one disgruntled nurse muttered behind my mother's back when she was caring for Eric as a baby, "She has Fifth Avenue airs and a First Avenue pocketbook." She was pretty close to the truth. As our family grew, however, we became more comfortable, like so many other beneficiaries of that post-World War II boom. In our case, the prosperity was supplemented, as I noted earlier, by the inheritance that Dad received from his Uncle Ed Bayles and the added income that Mom brought in through The Maizie Shop.

Scarsdale, New York, was no ordinary suburb. Situated 22 miles due north of New York City, in the heart of lower Westchester County, it had a reputation for class, comfort, and convenience. There in 1772, Hessian mercenaries under the command of General De Heister advanced against the Americans and a battle had been fought within a couple of hundred yards of the house where I grew up. George Washington himself was pursued up the old Post Road by General Howe, again within yards of where our modest stucco Tudor-style home was later built. But by the mid-twentieth century Scarsdale was a fast growing township of attractive houses, excellent schools, and three tidy villages.

Scarsdale drew many migrants from the City, drawn by its leafy streets and pleasant public places. It especially attracted Jews looking for a better life, who wanted to leave behind the old enclaves of Brooklyn or Manhattan, and were anxious that their children receive the best available public education. When I grew up there, it was about 50% Jewish and 50% Gentile. The two groups lived in overlapping spheres until the children reached puberty. Once puberty set in, they separated into their own social groups, joined their own country clubs, and attended their own "Y's"—either the YMCA or the YMHA as the case may be.

I thought almost nothing of this subtle divide because many of my childhood friends and neighbors were Jews. In fact, some of them celebrated Christian holidays pretty much as we did. The Steins, whose daughter Ginger was a special friend of mine from childhood, had Christmas parties replete with decorated trees, presents, eggnog, and Christmas carols. Many decades later at a school reunion I asked Ginger how this came to be. She had a ready answer that I had not considered. "You have to remember that we German Jews were all about assimilation." Of course, some Jews, especially those escaping the growing terror in Germany between the two World Wars, came to America (as had Ginger's grandparents) intending to leave behind their overt Jewish customs and embrace the new world with a vengeance. However, even Ginger, to whom I was attracted at all of 14, was squirreled away to an essentially all-Jewish country club just at the time when my interest might have blossomed into something more serious.

JEWS AND GENTILES

There was a dark side to this Jewish/Gentile divide, invisible though it might have been to the casual observer. Certain clubs were not open to Jews. Our family friends, the Landauers, had three beautiful daughters. Our two families would gather for supper together and then riotously play "The Game," that is, charades. But Jim Landauer was a Jew, and though he had graduated from Dartmouth and mingled quite freely in Gentile social circles, he was not able to join the unprepossessing Fox Meadow Tennis Club where we all played and socialized. Jim's wife was a strikingly beautiful blonde, and clearly Gentile. Their daughters took after their mother. However, there was an ugly and painful incident when one of the daughters had a birthday party and invited all her friends. Rumor has it that not one of them had turned up. Whether that is the exact story, I do not at this date know, but in some way she was made to feel that she did not belong.

It is to the great credit of the then rector of St. James the Less, the church in which I was reared, that he broke the grip of this prejudice on our town. A young girl from the parish was expected to make her debut at a cotillion at the Scarsdale Golf Club, an all-Gentile institution. She chose as her escort a boy from the St. James youth group, who happened to be a convert from Judaism to Christianity. How serious a convert I do not know; but he was a member of the church who happened to have an obviously Jewish name.

The Committee on Escorts discovered this infringement of Club policy and forbade the girl to bring her friend as her escort. At this point, the Rector entered the fray. He essentially excommunicated all church members on the Committee of Escorts, telling them that they would not be welcome at Holy Communion until they had made their peace with God. In other words, they would have to change their policy. The incident hit the news wires, and even resulted in a spread in *LIFE* Magazine. The Bishop of New York supported the Rector, and by the time the dust settled, Scarsdale was a very different place.

But Scarsdale was sometimes portrayed in a more unfavorable light. During the upheavals of the Sixties, a very critical article on Scarsdale appeared in *LIFE*, titled: "You have to have grown up in Scarsdale to know how bad it is." It reflected the disappointment among a younger generation, eager for fundamental social change, which judged Scarsdale to have sold out to bourgeois materialist values. No wonder the kids were rebelling, though against what it is not always easy to determine. It may have been their parents' own lack of moral compass.

My generation, however, grew up in the Forties and Fifties, a time that Christian thinker Os Guinness dubbed "the bland leading the bland." Ours was a calmer era. We were the children of what has been called "the great generation." Our parents were that generation of men (and women) who sacrificed all to stem the tide of fascist oppression. They had returned home to start families and rebuild America into the economic powerhouse it became.

AN AMERICAN IN EUROPE

When it came time to apply to college, I had several advantages. My father had attended Yale, and my brother was then attending. Moreover, in those days Yale drew very heavily from the leading private boarding and day schools up and down the East Coast, especially those in New England. I was told that my headmaster simply called the Admissions Head at Yale and said: "I have eleven boys for you this year." Imagine that! Mr. Barber instructed me not to bother applying anywhere else, so I didn't. Of course, there were College Board exams to take, and my grades at St. Mark's were acceptable, though not exceptional. Nevertheless, I got into Yale easily, and in the fall of 1954 set my sights toward New Haven.

The summer just before my matriculation at Yale was a dream come true for a person who was, like me, afflicted with a high degree of wanderlust. From a young age I had yearned to travel, and even plastered my prep school walls with travel posters from all over the world, especially Europe. So, when I got the chance to become a summer exchange student with the American Field Service (AFS), I jumped. The AFS had originally started as an ambulance service during World War II, but after the war, it morphed into a student exchange movement. Its head was Dr. Stephen Galatti. Galatti was both a graduate and a trustee of St. Mark's. I knew him slightly from his occasional presence on campus for board meetings, and that may be how I was given truly a sweetheart deal that summer.

I was to spend two months in France—the first with the family of a French exchange student who had spent one year in the class ahead of me at St. Mark's, and the second with Mme Levy-Despas of Paris and St. Tropez. I already knew the French student, Francois-Henri Ballande, and so July proved to be a soft landing into a very unfamiliar culture. I tried my best to speak French; but Francois-Henri's family would always reply to me in English. As a result, what French I was able to practice I learned from Francois-Henri's little sister who was the one member of the family who spoke simply and slowly enough for me to understand.

The most notable experience of that first month was a five-day bike trip that Francois-Henri, his younger brother Jean-Pierre and I took throughout Provence. We fought traffic along the coastal road for a few days, and then headed inland to the Gorges de Verdun. I was riding a Velo Moteur, a kind of motorized bicycle that required pedaling when going uphill. Francois-Henri and Jean-Pierre were on regular bicycles. Other than a night spent on the beach, being ferociously attacked by mosquitoes, and another in a remote utility hut on the side of the mountain highway, that we broke into in order to take shelter from a vicious storm, the trip was notable for the food that the boys had brought along: saucisson and tomatoes. Saucisson is a grisly, hard, sausage that wants to be chewed raw. I had been exposed to this unfamiliar form of food in Paris at the start of my journey, and detested it. But surprise, surprise: there in our bags was a full 5-day supply of the stuff. By the end of the trip, driven by hunger, I managed to like it.

It was that second month, spent in a seaside villa in St. Tropez that proved most memorable. Mme Levy-Despas had been married and later divorced from the Coca-Cola "king" of France. She was from an aristocratic French family, and had a formidable mansion on the Left Bank in Paris. Her former husband was a Jew. Their only child, Guy Levy-Despas, was therefore half Jewish. When the Nazis threatened to overtake France, Madame and her son Guy fled to Canada. They lived through the war in Montreal, and Guy enrolled in Amherst College in Western Massachusetts. Upon graduation, Guy (pronounced "Gee" with a gutteral G) enlisted in the Royal Canadian Air Force and was shot down and killed in a mission over Malta in the Mediterranean.

Overcome with grief, Madame vowed to always wear his wings and dress in black, which she managed to do very fashionably for the rest of her life. She also instituted a scholarship for a deserving French student to attend Amherst each year. So, in any given year, one could find four Levy-Despas scholars at Amherst. A statue in memory of Guy still stands in the garden of one of Amherst's fraternity houses.

In addition, Madame took in an AFS student each summer—most of whom, curiously, were headed to Yale. So imagine all these French students plus that summer's AFS student in addition to an amazing ménage of guests literally filling her St. Tropez estate throughout the summer season.

Les Greniers, as her place was named, had been commandeered by the Nazis as their regional headquarters during the War. Now refurbished, with a small guesthouse for all the young men she invited to visit, *Les Greniers* was filled with summer invitees whose particulars read like a page from a Flaubert novel. There was His Excellence General Peshkov, the son of the noted Russian author Maxim Gorky. He had lost an arm fighting for the French Foreign Legion, and wore the Croix de Guerre, one of the highest of French medals. There was Lady Helenea van der Zay from Istanbul and Amsterdam. There was Count Colona, of Corsican heritage, whose Jaguar's tires we managed to deflate one evening as a prank. There also was Elizabeth de la Rochefoucauld, descendant from the famous author of *Maxim Morales*, and others of equal standing.

Lunch and dinner were served in a huge dining room overlooking the Mediterranean, where the elegance of the fare was augmented by lively conversation, much of which I was beginning to understand, including some very dirty jokes that I was not supposed to understand! My impression of this lot of petty nobility was that they were bored, slightly degenerate, mostly irreligious, and yet personally quite attractive. In August, I explored the delights of St. Tropez, a town that had recently hit the international headlines because of the presence of celebrities like film star Brigitte Bardot. St. Tropez unquestionably had the finest beaches on the whole Cote D'Azur.

In a gesture of friendship, Elizabeth de la Rochefoucauld, who managed to appear at every dinner with a different color cigarette holder that matched her outfit, gave me a copy of her ancestor's *Maxims Morales.* Inside was the inscription: "lisez mon aieul, mais arrosez le tout de soleil de St. Tropez" which, loosely translated means: "Read my ancestor, but soak up all the sun of St. Tropez."

One memorable incident during that stay was the reenactment in nearby Frejus of the Allied landing in Provence in the summer of 1944. We all sat in bleachers under the hot August sun while rank after rank of soldiers from each country that had participated in the invasion marched before us. The US Marines came last and literally gleamed in the sunshine with their dazzling chrome helmets. Meanwhile, out in the harbor a dozen or more warships came as close to land as they could. As an American surrounded by Europeans, I felt justifiably proud of my country's role in that war, and as I write now more than a half a century later, I realize how close to the actual events of that invasion I was in 1954. A mere decade separated us! Years later, in 2007, I revisited the Riviera with my son David. He, at the age of 20, caught some of the pathos of it all when we visited the American cemetery in nearby Draginaun. Row after tow of white crosses (interspersed with some stars of David) reminded us of the sacrifice of those courageous U.S. servicemen.

I also remember from that amazing summer the round-trip Atlantic crossing in a converted old military vessel, The MS *Seven Seas*. The voyage lasted a full ten days each way from New York to Le Havre and back. It felt like we were taking a "slow boat to China," and when the inevitable storm came, we popped atop some very stormy waves like a cork adrift on the sea. Home again, with a truly exotic summer behind me, I was catapulted into my freshman year at Yale.

CHAPTER 5

UNIVERSITY YEARS

YALE

Yale in the fall of 1954 was, of course, still an all-male institution. Moreover it was predominantly "preppy", that is about 60% of all the incoming freshmen had prepared at one of the prestigious independent schools. They brought with them a unique sense of entitlement gained on the playing fields of Hotchkiss, Deerfield, or Penn Charter. Along with them was an assortment of total newcomers to the heady world of the Ivy League. I recall one who had been a valedictorian from a high school in Lancaster, PA. His parents had outfitted him with all the "wrong" clothes. Another was the son of a Pentecostal evangelist from Little Rock, Arkansas (Bob Sellers, who later became a lifelong friend). Still another was a football hero from a high school in Tacoma, Washington. All were quickly initiated into a social world that eventually separated the privileged minority destined to become members of exclusive secret societies like Skull and Bones, Berzelius or Book and Snake, and the rest who, though still Yalies, were to make their own way as best they could.

Like Oxford and Cambridge, Yale features residential colleges that provide not only living quarters but also dining facilities, libraries, and seminar rooms for some small classes. Much of one's social life takes place in the residential college to which one is assigned. I was assigned to Timothy Dwight, named for the illustrious president of Yale and grandson of Jonathan Edwards. At the end of the eighteenth century his preaching and teaching had initiated the Second Great Awakening.

In the mid 1950's, Yale was a victim of the confident secularism that breathed spiritual death, like halitosis, into the academic environment. University chaplains such as the avuncular Sidney Lovett maintained a good face, and tried to keep students interested in religion with courses that essentially taught liberal Protestantism. His students dubbed his key course "cokes, smokes and dirty jokes." But the telltale sign that the 1950's were a low ebb in the religious life on campus was the pathetic church attendance by undergraduates. If ten percent of them sought out a church on any given Sunday morning, I would have been surprised. Bill Buckley hit the nail on the head with his 1951 analysis, *God and Man at Yale.* He rightly claimed in his best-seller that Yale faculty were actively forcing a liberal ideology on students. In my experience, it was open season in many classes on anything approaching orthodox religious belief. Students, if they did have faith, kept quiet about it, eventually replacing it with trendy *avant-garde* notions of individuality and self-expression.

As undergraduates we all learned to sing *Boola Boola* and wave white handkerchiefs during the last few minutes of the Harvard-Yale football game (when Yale was winning). We traveled to Smith and Mt. Holyoke in search of female friendship. We squirreled ourselves away in the study carrels of the Harkness Memorial Library, and we hunkered down at exams to make up for lost time.

In September of 1954 I arrived at Yale as a new but committed believer in Jesus Christ. I was also confident of the integrity of the Bible's witness to him. This put me in a small, unique group of freshmen that was willing to admit to an evangelical orientation. Of a thousand incoming freshmen in my class of '58, there were probably only four or five of us who were willing to be so defined. Today the number of incoming Christians with overt evangelical beliefs has much increased at places like Yale, due in large part to the growing number of African-American, Asian, and public high school students entering. I would like to think also that vigorous youth movements like FOCUS, have helped. But I will tell that story later. In my day, however, the four or five of us who would so define ourselves stood out, especially since we were unashamedly trying to win others to a similar faith—part of the evangelical impulse that had certainly found its match in sophisticated Yale.

Yale Christian Fellowship (YCF)

Remnants of a more vigorous Christian witness on the Yale campus remained, especially in buildings or other monuments named for illustrious graduates or faculty who had led revivals in the past. But in my day the university had fallen prey to the corrosive theological skepticism advanced by theologians like Paul Tillich who, in an effort to be relevant to the current culture, had "translated" terms like God into "ground of being." To him and other noted theologians, God was more a subjective sense of connectedness to the life force, or as Friedrich Schleiermacher had put it "the whence of our religious emotions", than the all-personal and all-powerful One who stands outside of the natural order and is willing to hear and answer prayer.

The Yale Christian Fellowship was not only a center of biblical orthodoxy, very much marginalized by the chaplains and religious luminaries on campus, but it was a place where one could find real faith and lasting friendships. I recall that Dietrich Bonhoeffer, a generation earlier, had found real faith during his days at the ultra-liberal Union Seminary in New York by attending a Baptist church in Harlem and a fundamentalist church on Broadway. In my freshman year, the YCF was a small, struggling student group affiliated with the national movement known as Inter-Varsity Christian Fellowship. Because it tried to be relevant to the spiritual needs of students, it did not represent itself as a plant by an off-campus, outside organization. Unlike Campus Crusade for Christ, which began its Yale ministry a couple of decades later, IVCF stressed on-campus student leadership as opposed to off-campus staff leadership. Consequently, our small group set about starting Bible study groups in our own dormitories, and witnessing vigorously among our friends and classmates. We even took the bold step of reserving time on the Yale Broadcasting Station for a 15-minute slot each evening that we called "Quiet Time". The title sounds a bit quaint today, I'm sure. But it was appropriate then. During that radio program, one of us would testify or share thoughts from the Bible in the hopes that some students might tune in. I also was invited to share my my faith journey and experience in print in the *Yale Daily News.* Another freshman (curiously, a former St. Mark's classmate of mine) wrote a parallel column sharing his revulsion at religion, "We have to be fair, guys."

During my college years, YCF grew from approximately 20 students (a few female nursing students from the Medical School would occasionally join us) to about 50. We could anticipate larger numbers from time to time when an outside speaker was scheduled. But the heart of our common life was a small prayer meeting that took place at 10 PM each evening in the gothic chapel that formed the base of Harkness Memorial Tower. There five to ten of us would gather for informal, extempore prayer. The meeting provided a vital safety valve for pent-up frustrations and a setting where lasting friendships were forged.

One of the great assets of YCF's connection with Inter-Varsity was the IVCF New England Director, Peter Haile. He would travel to meet with us at least once a term from his base in the Boston area. In addition to the Ivy-League schools, he covered a host of other institutions for Inter-Varsity. Peter was an Oxford-educated Englishman, who brought what we would today call "street cred" to any group of undergraduates we might gather. Gentle, firmly rooted in his Christ-centered spirituality, warm and personable, Peter cut an image that was light years away from the stereotypical grinning, wide-tie, zoot-suited Bible-pounding preacher many had come to identify with American evangelicalism. With a cultured Southern wife, Jane, who later became a well-known charismatic teacher, Peter quickly took me into his circle of Inter-Varsity friends.

In 1955, at Peter's suggestion, I spent July at IVCF's "Campus in the Woods"—a secluded island campus located in Ontario's Lake of Bays. While there, I was introduced to Pioneer Camps, and to Canadian evangelicals with whom I later reconnected when I became Rector of Toronto's Little Trinity Church in my fifties.

One memory of my first night at Campus-in-the-Woods stands out. There were students from colleges I had never heard of, and would normally have looked down upon, given my elite vantage point. But I learned a lesson in faith from them. Most, it turned out, had simply trusted God to provide the finances for their summer experience. That evening, one by one, they shared their gratitude for how God had provided the funds that enabled them to attend. A check would unexpectedly turn up in the mailbox. A friend would slip them a few dollars. As I reflected on my own experience, all I had done was either write a check myself or ask Mom or Dad to do so. That night I saw how my comfortable suburban lifestyle had insulated me from some of the rougher aspects of life, and had deprived me of the opportunity to learn important lessons in trusting God.

College life in those days tended to be apolitical. That changed a decade later when the Viet Nam War consumed so many students' attention, especially at Yale which hosted Chaplain Bill Coffin's radical activism. We wore "I Like Ike" buttons, in support of General Dwight Eisenhower's campaign for the presidency, in the Fifties and were happy to let the world go by. Only the mounting arms race with the Soviets, creating the possibility of a nuclear holocaust troubled us; but that seemed like a remote possibility. Moreover, evangelical Christianity had only just begun to come out of the social ghetto into which the fundamentalist/modernist controversies of the early twentieth century over the authority and inspiration of the Bible had driven it. The controversy pitted liberals who brought their historical skepticism to the text of the Bible, and rejected the miraculous, against conservatives (dubbed fundamentalists) who sought to adhere to its literal and intended meaning. But the next several decades were to see a remarkable growth of evangelical Protestantism and along with it a corresponding expansion of missions. But all that was frankly hard to envision from our limited vantage point as a small struggling student campus group that seemed at the time so out of step with the mainstream culture in which we found ourselves.

BILLY GRAHAM

All this began to change with Billy Graham's mission to Yale in the winter of 1957. Each year the University sponsored a mission, in which the chaplains were actively involved. The missions tended to reflect the varying theological trends emanating from the major divinity schools, of which Yale's own Divinity School was a noted trend-setter. So, these missioners were usually gifted preachers; some even had a slight tinge of evangelistic vision. Nevertheless, on the key theological points, they were all decidedly liberal.

One exception was James K. Pike. Pike was then Dean of the Cathedral of St. John the Divine in New York City, and author of *The Church's Faith*, a relatively orthodox expression of Anglican Christianity. Pike's personal style was decidedly pugnacious, and his personal manner exuded self-importance. But his answers to questions, at that point in his life, tended to be surprisingly orthodox. Later he became a flaming radical denying most of the tenets of the Faith. Pike, who had come in the winter of 1955, was followed in 1956 by another Anglican, the British evangelist, Bryan Green. Vigorously distancing himself from any whiff of Fundamentalism, Green—although Christ-centered, and personally attractive—missed a golden opportunity to proclaim Christ that year, in my opinion. But by then, Billy Graham had risen to international prominence.

And so it was, bowing to pressure from the YCF, and to a sense of inevitability, I suppose, the University stuck its collective neck out and invited Billy Graham to come in the winter of 1957. Assistant chaplains were chosen to balance out the theological thrust of what they greatly feared he might say. Many of them doubtless still thought of Graham as a theologically naïve backwoods preacher. I recall overhearing one of these chaplains express great worry at this possibility. But he then acknowledged that when Graham talked about sin he wasn't really all that far from what his clergy friends and he had learned from Reinhold Niebuhr, the great neo-orthodox icon!

In the winter of 1957, just a few months prior to his remarkable 1957 New York Crusade that was scheduled to last a couple of weeks, but went on for nearly three months, Graham arrived at Yale. We in the YCF were praying up a storm, totally immersed in the anticipated event.

Each night the crowds grew, as more and more curious undergraduates were drawn to the meetings. The *Yale Daily News* provided blow-by-blow coverage of the events, and even now, more than a half-century later, it is regarded by most members of my Class of 1958 as one of the key events of our undergraduate life. The final night of his mission was life-changing for me. I was seated on the stage of the fully packed Woolsey Hall, as a member of the invitation committee, and therefore had a ringside seat from which to view the student reaction to Graham's appeal for a decision for Christ. I watched audience members' attitude change from cynicism to interest, and then to conviction. When the call for commitment was made, and when those willing to commit their lives to Christ were asked to stand, many did so. As we all bowed our heads and prayed, I quickly scanned the crowd that was standing. What I saw was not what I would have expected: Instead of a smattering of Yale's quiet Midwestern contingent, I saw dozens of East Coast students standing, many of whom had gone to leading private schools prior to Yale. I was stunned. These students had seemed to me among the least interested in religion, and certainly the ten classmates that came to New Haven with me from St. Mark's fell into that category. But here, before my eyes, with 300 souls standing was evidence of deep spiritual hunger that no amount of drunken binges at Jimmy Ryan's bar in New York, or erotic escapades at Smith or Wellesley, could satisfy.

One of those whose life would be dramatically changed through the preaching of Graham was Ned Hale. Ned was a Taft graduate whose roommates had done a bit of bed tumbling with Jane Fonda during her Vassar College days. He made his decision for Christ the following summer during the New York Crusade. Ostensibly a party-going, happy-go-lucky guy who hadn't given the deeper questions of life much thought, Ned's faith took hold and he never looked back. He spent almost all of his working life in student ministry with Inter-Varsity Christian Fellowship and with his devoted wife Sharon brought up a brood of creative Christian children.

Almost as if to undo the "damage done" by Graham the following year, 1958, the powers that be invited Charles (Chuck) Templeton, a Canadian evangelist whom the National Council of Churches had been promoting as liberal Protestantism's "answer" to Billy Graham. Effective, buoyant, and racy, Templeton ploughed through a series of talks that left one scratching one's head. I was in no way surprised when like Bishop James K. Pike in later life he openly abandoned his orthodox faith, and became a thoroughgoing skeptic.

JOHN STOTT

The awareness that many of my Yale classmates were more interested in Christianity than they seemed to be coincided with a casual comment Peter Haile, our Inter-Varsity staff worker, made to me: "Peter, you are a typical 'Bash camper'." Naturally, I asked him what that meant, and he coyly replied: "You'll find out some day." With that stimulus, I began a quiet search for the meaning of the phrase 'Bash camper.' Various English friends, including one professor to whom

I was close, gave their answers. But none had the faintest idea what the term meant. Then the Rev. John Stott came to Yale as a follow-up speaker to the 1957 Graham mission. Stott, then in his thirties, was a rising star in the evangelical sky. He had graduated from Rugby School; where he had been "head boy", and then gone on to gain a double first at Cambridge in Modern Languages and Theology. The full story of his life is now told in a large two-volume biography by the Rt. Rev. Timothy Dudley-Smith, a British bishop, and in a growing series of additional biographies. But for the purposes of my story, it is significant that when the *New York Times* was asked who was the most influential leader in the evangelical world of the second half of the twentieth century, Columnist David Brooks named John Stott. John Stott died on July 27, 2011 at 90, and was mourned the world over. A huge memorial service was held in his honor at St. Paul's Cathedral, London, for which tickets were required. It was one of the great privileges of my life to have spent 40 quiet minutes at his bedside in England just six weeks before he died.

Stott had forsaken military service in the Forties because of pacifist tendencies—much to the chagrin of his father, a distinguished Harley Street physician who had been knighted. During those war years the young Stott had become the right hand man to Rev. Eric Nash. Nash, nicknamed "Bash" by almost everyone, was a bachelor clergyman who for years had implemented a vision to reach England's leading private schoolboys for God. He had done this through a series of vacation house parties, called "camps", that to this day continue to impact the lives of privileged English boys (and now girls) attending independent schools. Curiously, in England these private schools are known as "public schools", one of the many anomalies of our language that prompted someone to quip: "America and England are two countries separated by a common language."

After ordination, Stott became Rector of All Soul's Church, Langham Place—a large parish next to the BBC and just up from Oxford Circus in the heart of London' fashionable shopping district. There he preached extraordinarily lucid biblical sermons and wrote books, more than forty of which are still in print to this day. Many of his books have been widely translated, and royalties from all his writings go towards the education of Christian pastors in the developing world. In addition to his writing, Stott led university missions in England and around the world—including America. That winter in 1957 he happened to be touring the USA, holding university missions. Thus it was the good fortune of the Yale Christian Fellowship to welcome him to New Haven as a follow-up to the Graham mission.

While Stott drew nothing like the crowds that Graham drew, on each of three evenings in the Yale Law School auditorium he sought to build a solid foundation under the Christian faith of many of those who had been touched only a couple of weeks previously. He was billeted in a Timothy Dwight College guest room, near my own rooms, giving me the opportunity to get to know him at that time. Since he was a leading Church of England figure and also an evangelical Christian with a deep and scholarly knowledge of the Bible, I plied him with questions that I had been storing up in my mind. He was the answer to my sophomoric attempt to build a bridge between the seemingly hostile worlds of Anglicanism and evangelicalism.

Of course I asked John Stott if he knew what a "Bash camper" was. Not only did he tell me the inside story about the Bash camps, which he knew so well, but he invited me to spend the summer in London as a kind of "intern" at All Souls. While the invitation was intriguing, I needed to postpone my answer for another year. But he whetted my appetite for a much fuller exposure to the Christian landscape of England, and especially to the Anglican evangelical aspect of it. Plus I was eager to learn all that I could about Bash and his unique ministry.

COLLEGE LIFE

Timothy Dwight College at Yale was unfortunately on a far edge of what had become a very urban campus. "We are the closest (residential) college to Paris" was the humorous way our college's Dean welcomed us to our lonely outpost. I decided to avoid fraternity life, as all but a small percentage of undergraduates at Yale did. However, I played on the freshman tennis team, sang in the freshman glee club, jogged in the Grove Street Cemetery, and played squash with my roommates. I also took menial jobs because neither of my parents supported me financially during my final two years.

I owned a grand old Buick sedan in those days—a gift from my grandparents. Bomp had procured it right after World War II from his brother, who was a Buick dealer in Nashville. It was one of the first cars to roll off the assembly line after the war. It sported a deliciously raucous blue-green color that caused the family to dub it the "beauty queen." Fortunately, by the time I took it to New Haven, it had been repainted a metallic gray. The Buick became a prized possession that enabled me to squire students here and there to conferences and sporting events.

Academically, I found Yale somewhat challenging. I had to speed up my reading skills, and my grades on the whole were acceptable but not noteworthy. I took Greek, which I felt led to take, suspecting that I would go on to seminary. However the university insisted that I study classical Greek rather than go up the hill to the Divinity School and learn *koine* (that is, biblical) Greek. But several courses, particularly those I took on the history of art and architecture, were fascinating. Long nights in various Yale libraries were peacefully ended by our daily prayer meeting held at 10 PM. This elegant chapel with an impressive fan vaulted ceiling would later become a Buddhist prayer space. But in our day it was a refuge from the competitive, secular, boozy dorm life that passed for "fun" in those days. I met Baptists from Texas, Methodists from Georgia, Pentecostals from Arkansas, and Bible Presbyterians from Seattle. These guys were totally unfamiliar with the New York suburban Episcopalianism in which I had been reared, and I found their backgrounds equally strange. But over time, we grew together, became a "band of brothers," supported one another, and reached out to the campus in a way that actually bore some fruit. Fifty years later our small YCF group returned to the Yale campus for a happy reunion.

By the time I graduated from Yale, having majored in American Studies to get as broad a liberal arts education as possible, I was looking for a way to put my fragmented family life behind me. I had a growing conviction that I should pursue theological study, but was not ready for a typical three-year American seminary experience. After all, I was just twenty-two and had no definite aspirations towards ordination, nor did I sense a clear call in that direction. Furthermore, I had not come to terms with my Episcopal Church upbringing, finding few if any American models that combined evangelical theology with Anglican churchmanship. My churchgoing during college had been confined to smaller evangelical churches like the Evangelical Free Church of New Haven where the Bible was preached in a dull, uninspiring way, but with a faithfulness to the text that was unmistakably authentic. Among my acquaintances only John Stott seemed to connect the two worlds in which my feet were firmly planted.

CHAPTER 6

DISINTEGRATING FAMILY

PAIN AND LOSS

Children rarely see the divorce of their parents coming. Certainly Eric and I, offstage at boarding school and college, did not anticipate what was coming between our mother and father. Only at the conclusion of my freshman year, in the spring of 1955, as the two of us drove home from New Haven to Scarsdale did we venture to talk about our parents' marriage with deepening concern. Then it all happened with mounting rapidity—and with sad and disastrous results.

A couple of days after our arrival home Dad took Eric and me for a short drive at which time he told us that he was moving out and that he and Mom were going to get a legal separation. At first we didn't believe that this would lead to divorce. After all, we were the "perfect happy family," weren't we? However, Dad did move out, and we comforted our mother in her grief and shame as best we could.

On reflection, she should have seen this coming, because she had done more than she should to bring it on. Someone who would separate herself as totally as she had done from her mate, who had retreated into a new world of non-stop church-going, who had sung hymns around the house in ways that could only annoy, and who had heaped condemnation on those who were unwilling to follow her path was, as we sometimes say, "asking for it." However, it still stung. Both Eric and I felt her pain; but when she condemned me because I would not adopt her unyielding attitude towards my father, the situation became intolerable.

It would be wrong to give the impression that my break with my mother was sudden. I felt a great deal of sympathy for her, knowing that the path that she had chosen to walk was a very lonely one indeed. True, she had made it worse. But, the fact that she was a woman who carried her feelings on her sleeve, and now had a husband who had abandoned her living in the same community where both had such a rich social life made her life extremely hard. The lack of support from her wider family only complicated matters.

My situation was awkward. I wanted to affirm the fact that I shared the same faith as my mother and brother, although I tried to temper it with what I hoped was a more graceful attitude towards those who did not see it our way. The three of us tried to stand together. For example, during the summer of 1956, after my sophomore year, Eric and I held Bible studies in our house at 24 Rugby Lane. A remarkable number of friends came, including searching skeptics. Sometimes, 35 young people would crowd into our living room. One who came, and later confessed Christ, was Don Martin from Tarrytown. Don was a Yale classmate of mine who went on to become a highly respected doctor. Later he credited his turning to Christ to the summer Bible studies in our house.

That summer also I also left to be a camp counselor at Pioneer Camp in Ontario. There I oversaw a tentful of impressionable 12 year-olds, and got to know other counselors from American and Canadian universities. There were moments of levity when several of us brought down the house during talent night with an impersonation in drag of the Andrews Sisters—a sexy tight-harmony vocal group that had been popular a decade earlier. In addition I enjoyed running the water-skiing boat on the camp's Clearwater Lake.

Looking back, over that difficult summer, it seems that an invisible hand was guiding my life and giving me, in faraway Canada, a respite from the pain I had left behind. Each evening after supper I typed a letter to my father, in an effort to help him understand the faith that my mother, brother and I shared. Later he took my very long letter to my grandmother, and she had it typeset and printed. I still have a copy. Little did I know that summer that I would later discover many of Canada's treasures, and invest a whole decade of my life in its future.

Back at Yale in the fall of 1957, with Eric, doing a one-year internship in a traveling student ministry, I threw myself into college life. That Thanksgiving I attempted to bring a young South African friend home for the break. I got no response to several letters home, and finally received a phone call that left me stunned.

My mother gave me an ultimatum: if I returned to my home I would be shunned. Why? Because I would not join her in labeling my father as a man who was rebelling against God. In an attempt to straddle the two increasingly separate worlds of my parents, I had become odious to both. I recall saying to my mother: "I'll be home to collect my belongings."

A good friend from Scarsdale, Betsy Ashton, who was attending Smith College, helped me pack my bags when I returned home that one last time from Yale. I can only imagine how the whole business soured Betsy to the evangelicalism in which she had been reared. I sadly said goodbye to my stone-faced mother, and moved to the third floor of my grandparents' house, a mile away. The whole incident remains extraordinarily painful in my memory; but as with so many domestic tragedies, this was not to be the last chapter in our family life. After I gained some personal distance from it all, I realized how deeply hurt my mother had been by the divorce. I could see that she was pleading for support through the only means she knew: threats, withdrawals, judgments, and (hidden from me) tears. I remain convinced that she had been misled by older Christian counselors and friends, and that the distorted, grace-less legalism that characterized too much of her spiritual journey at that point was an outward expression of a troubled woman who had experienced one of the most traumatic rejections a woman could bear. Sadly, only once many years later, do I recall seeing my parents in the same room. It was at the wedding of Ruth Moore, my brother's middle daughter. The wedding and reception were held on the campus of the Cardigan Mountain School in Canaan, New Hampshire, and Dad and his new wife Betsy Larned Davidson Moore came. I watched as he and Mom danced—somewhat awkwardly—during the reception. Mom looked lovely. The dance was clearly an obligatory performance, and it signaled nothing in the way of an even partial reconciliation. But through the years when I visited him, Dad would often ask after "your mother." And on her side, Mom would later tell me that she held no ill-will towards Dad.

ESCAPE

Some would argue that the divorce of my parents was the cause of my "late" marriage at the ripe old age of 32. Certainly I was more cautious than some in my relationship with women, having seen the breakup of what on the surface appeared to be a happy marriage. I was therefore unlikely to give my heart to someone who might break it. But, I think the real reasons lay more in the fact that by the time I began to look seriously for a wife, I was already ordained and knew instinctively that whomever I married would be asked to live a very different life than many other women and would need to share something of the same vocation to which I was being called.

The divorce of my parents, and my subsequent banishment from my own home, left me essentially without a family at the age of twenty. I continued to live at my grandparents' home, but found reasons to be away from Scarsdale as much as possible. Summers were spent in a variety of service occupations or on one occasion traveling across country by car with an IVCF staff worker to his home in Tacoma, Washington, to explore the West and spend time with like-minded friends.

I recall that western journey as special. I water-skied in frigid Puget Sound, hiked on Mt. Rainier, took ferry rides to Victoria, British Columbia, picked vegetables in the Yakima Valley (to earn some money), and met noted Christians like Dave and Annette Weyerhaeuser, of the famous lumber family. At the end of that summer I returned to the East Coast via Pasadena, taking a Greyhound bus down the Coast, stopping in San Francisco and viewing Big Sur along the way. Pasadena was dry, hot, and like the rest of Los Angeles covered with a haze that stung the eyes and made driving on its freeways almost impossible. However, there I saw Fuller Seminary. At the time, I was immature enough to dismiss Fuller as a mere Bible school founded by the folksy Charles E. Fuller whose radio program "The Old Fashioned Revival Hour" had turned me off. Little did I know that Fuller would become one of the largest and most respectable evangelical seminaries in the country, and that I would pursue my own Doctor of Ministry degree there in the late 1980s.

Somehow, losing a family opened me up to realize the richness of Christian friendship. Not only did family members such as the redoubtable Aunt Peg step into the breach, inviting me to join her and Uncle Ed on a Christmas trip to Mexico in 1957, but many other Christian families welcomed me into their homes and lives. There were the Sibleys, for example. "Mom and Pop" Sibley presided over a small Baptist church on the edge of one of New Haven's less desirable neighborhoods. God had apparently put into their hearts a deep compassion for Yale students, and so they would regularly invite us to their house for Sunday dinner—even though we did not attend their church. On special occasions, such as a birthday, they would insist on my bringing friends with me, and I was thus introduced to the graciousness of caring Christian people from a social spectrum I had never encountered before. These encounters, where Christ's presence was almost palpable in the most humble surroundings, could not have been a more stark contrast than with the New York social scene, replete with gala dinners and glittering debutantes, that only a few years before had been the staple of my social life.

After the Christmas trip to Mexico with my aunt and uncle in December of '58 (at which I got the worst sunburn of my life), I flew to Urbana, Illinois to attend the triennial Missions Conference held by Inter-Varsity. More than 5,000 college students packed into the large covered stadium to hear speaker after speaker present the challenge of missionary work abroad. The final communion service was particularly moving, I recall, demonstrating that unity across denominations was not only possible, but was truly a gift from God in a day when denominations still held a great deal of sway, and people were divided into cliques rather than united in the one body. The Ecumenical Movement that blossomed during those years was the high water mark of American denominationalism in the 1960s.

It gained considerable visibility a decade later and was a bold effort to bridge these divisions. But the bridge was already being built by many para-church organizations that powerfully witnessed to a spiritual unity in Christ that transcended institutional boundaries.

BACK TO EUROPE

In the summer of 1958, as a volunteer chaperone for the AFS, I boarded the same rickety lumbering ex-military vessel that had transported me to Europe as an AFS student four years earlier, *The M.S. Seven Seas*. This time, however, we sailed from Montreal rather than New York. Seeking to put my faith into action, I tentatively put a sign on the ship's notice board that there would be a Bible study in the library each morning at 10:30 AM. Perhaps out of curiosity, or boredom, a handful of students showed up. Among them was a young girl from Karachi, Pakistan, who had grown up in a Zoroastrian family and spent her senior year of high school somewhere in the upper Midwest. Zoroastrianism is a relatively obscure religion, mostly confined to Iran and the Indian sub-continent. It combines Eastern and Western religious ideas, but holds to a supreme monotheism. This girl literally devoured our study of the New Testament and it was obvious that the person of Jesus captured her imagination. I gave her a pocket-sized New Testament at the end, and you would have thought I had given her gold. However, when we arrived in Le Havre, France and she preceded me down the gangplank to her waiting parents, there were no introductions. I learned from this experience how delicate is the task of what is commonly called "cross-cultural missions." I could see how exciting and yet controversial it is to share Christ with those who, because of background or geography, are almost totally ignorant of him. Little did I know that Christianity, until then largely perceived as a Western phenomenon, would soon grow so substantially in the developing world as to change its center of gravity from Europe and North America to the Global South.

Back once more on European soil, I found myself with a couple of months to kill before matriculating at Oxford University in the fall. The decision to attend Oxford, and "read" theology had not been a hard one. It afforded me the chance to learn at another of the great universities of the world, to pursue theology in a non-seminary context, and to prolong my undergraduate experience in a place where history, culture and learning literally oozed from the walls. I had been encouraged to go to Oxford by Peter Haile, and thanks in part to the support of his letter of commendation, I was admitted to his alma mater, Jesus College.

Needing wheels, I ordered a Lambretta motor scooter from Milan. Lambretta was soon-to-be locked into a deadly rivalry with Vespa, a rivalry that eventually Vespa won. But the mopeds each produced were equally useful, fun, and exciting to drive. Mine was a two-toned light blue.

Traveling alone in a foreign country has its compensations. While it is usually better to have at least one traveling companion, I found that being a solo traveler meant that I could meet local people and other tourists more easily. That happened in Milan. Since my scooter was not quite ready for delivery, I had a couple of days to kill, and so wandered around the city. One evening, viewing the Duomo (Milan's Cathedral), I struck up a conversation with a Dane named Eric. He was very sad, missing Copenhagen, because his wife had left him for another relationship. We talked freely as he unburdened himself to an eager listener. When Eric heard that I was eventually headed for Denmark in a couple of weeks, he hastily scribbled a note in Danish and stuffed it into my pocket. "Please give this to my family. They are very concerned for me." He said his family ran a bakery in downtown Copenhagen, and so I promised to pass on the note.

A couple of weeks later I was in his beloved city and, with a young Scottish student I had met in a local hostel, I headed downtown to find the bakery. Well, it was no mere bakery. It was a veritable emporium: ice cream, cakes, candy, and baked goods, all absolutely top of the line. When the family read the letter I passed on to them, they were overjoyed. Eric must have said something like: "Take good care of him." So we were seated at a table, and brought coffee, pastry, ice cream and tray after tray of sweets. It was a childhood dream come true. Remarkably, 54 years later in 2012, I was back in Copenhagen and at the age of 76 was riding around on a bicycle. Lo and behold, my traveling companion and I found the very establishment on a quiet side street and chatted with the new owner as he was closing up for the day. It was exactly as I remembered it. I even recalled the table where I had sat so many decades earlier.

My trip from Italy to Denmark in 1958 took me along the French Riviera where I made a quick stop in St. Tropez to once again visit Mme Levy-Despas and her ménage of illustrious guests. I was welcomed and briefly treated to a uniquely French summer experience on the Cote d'Azur. However, a few days later, while I was motoring along the north coast of Lake Geneva, a gust of wind from the Jura mountains swept me and the scooter off the road. Fortunately, the roadside grass was high, and neither my brand-new scooter nor I suffered serious injury. After a comforting night in a decent hotel, I was back on the road, headed for Heidelberg and an overnight train for Kiel. From Kiel I drove across the Danish border and after a couple of days in Copenhagen arrived in Hillerod a hamlet close to the historical Hamlet's castle, Kronberg Castle. The castle offers a commanding view of the body of water that separates Denmark from Sweden.

I was there to attend a conference sponsored by IFES, the International Fellowship of Evangelical Students. I particularly enjoyed meeting George Rawlyk, a Canadian Rhodes Scholar at Oxford. George went out of his way to make me welcome both at the conference and later in Oxford—where we each agreed to do our best to stop the other from picking up an English accent. It was only at the end of the conference that I discovered that George was engaged to Mary, another attendee at the conference. "But why, if you were engaged to Mary, did you spend so much time with me?" I asked him. His answer showed me something of the depths of his dedication. "Both Mary and I agreed," he said, "to concentrate on supporting other students, and to put our own relationship on hold until after the conference itself." Later George became a well-known professor of history at Queen's University in Ontario, and a highly-respected scholar.

From Denmark I headed down the coast of Holland on my way to England, somehow toting an oversized Dutch student and his suitcase on the back of my scooter. He had hitched a ride with me towards the lakes district of Holland where his family was on holiday. It turned out his parents and their friends were high-level Royal Dutch Shell executives, and their favorite resort turned out to be a real eye-popper. For a couple of days, he and I sailed around in the Friesland area of Holland before I bid him adieu and headed across the Channel to England.

LONDON

There to meet me as I pulled into London on my scooter was Desmond Dugan, John Stott's personal secretary—another bachelor with decidedly debonair tastes, and a firm Christian commitment. He took me to "the Rectory" at 12 Weymouth Street, W.1—a large, simple but very comfortable townhouse where John Stott and a houseful of curates, cooks, housekeepers, and assorted students lived in community.

I was welcomed warmly, but with a British sense of decorum. The house had its rules, and they had to be respected. John Stott was not to be disturbed. The curates had their daily schedules, and mealtimes were to be punctually kept. This was my first exposure to an Anglican Christian community where Jesus Christ was worshiped and the Bible taken to be the Word of God, but where British culture was observed scrupulously.

Most memorable among these deeply dedicated Anglican Christians who lived or worked at the Rectory was Packie—or Miss Packer, the matron. She was obviously well-educated, and functioned as a sort of mother confessor to two yet unmarried resident curates, as well as to almost anybody who came through. I sensed that John Stott himself would seek her counsel when troubled or perhaps just plain lonely. Packie was right out of a novel: one of those unique, crusty Englishwomen who would brook no nonsense from anybody, but who hid a very wise and tender heart behind a slightly gruff exterior.

I was given a tiny garret room on the 5th floor and would be welcomed there whenever I was "down" from Oxford during long vacations. The two curates became very good friends of mine. One, Julian Charley, was a bright academically oriented man with a warm smile and winsome ways. Later, well into his forties,

Julian married Clare and sired two children while becoming an Old Testament scholar, seminary professor, and author. He was an Anglican participant in ARCIC, the Joint Anglican/Roman Catholic International Theological Consultation. Over the succeeding decades Julian and Clare would become two of my favorite people to visit and spend time with on Sandra's and my many trips back to England.

The other curate was Geoffrey Rawlins. Like Julian, Geoff was a product of the "Bash camps." He was also a graduate of Cambridge. However, Geoff was from a more aristocratic background than Julian and combined a strong biblical piety with a love of art, antiques, and the finer things of life. To my delight, several years later Geoff came to the United States to work with me in the Council for Religion in Independent Schools as well as FOCUS. Geoff and I worked side-by-side for several years in these student ministries until I married, and Geoff decided that the world of landscape and portrait painting was to be his next career. He left New York for Italy to study under the famed Pietro Annigoni who in 1954 had painted a severe and controversial portrait of Queen Elizabeth II. Sadly, most of Geoff's friends totally lost touch with him (or vice versa) in the years to come.

HYDE PARK

On my very first Sunday in London, with time to kill, I ventured out along Oxford Street to Marble Arch. Every Sunday there a wide assortment of speakers would hold forth from box tops or make-shift platforms on almost any subject: politics and religion were favorites. Hecklers would stand as close to the speaker as possible and shout out troublesome questions, or make caustic comments to the merriment of the crowd. It was entertainment of a very rarefied and jovial sort.

That afternoon I was listening to a Salvation Army lassie preach her heart out. I noticed a young sailor standing nearby, listening intently. So I decided to have some fun: "What do you think of what she's saying?" I asked. "Oh, I don't believe any of it," he replied. "Why not?" I responded. Before long, a small crowd had gathered and we were engaged in an intense debate. I recall an elderly English lady on one side, and a young boy of about 13 on the other.

As we talked, a strange-looking man joined us. He was wearing a blue duffel coat that had blueprints spilling from a side pocket. He wore his hair page-boy style, which was unusual in the late 1950s. He told the sailor, "Young man, you ought to listen and not to speak," then walked away. Surprised at such support coming from a complete stranger, I went in search of the man as soon as our little group disbanded.

I found him at the edge of another crowd, and screwing up my courage walked up to him and said: "You look like an interesting man. What do *you* believe?" No matter how hard I pressed, I couldn't get a straight answer out of him. He seemed totally mysterious. Finally he looked at me and asked: "Young man, do you know the crown of glory?" "Well, yes, I said. I know *about* the crown of glory. Doesn't St. Paul talk about it as a reward for a life well-lived?" "I have seen the crown of glory in my Father's house," he replied. "You have seen the crown of glory in your Father's house?" I asked. "You don't claim to be Jesus Christ?" With piercing eyes, he said: "You have said it." Then he went on to upbraid me for my hardness of heart and my unbelief and walked away. You can imagine my surprise when, on my very first day in England I encountered a man who seriously claimed to be Jesus Christ.

THE RECTORY

The Rectory at 12 Weymouth Street gave me a bird's eye view of a bustling Anglican parish that was fast becoming known all over the world as a place for solid biblical exposition and creative parish-based evangelism. Everybody who was anybody, it seemed, came through All Souls in those days. So, through my growing friendship with John Stott, who insisted I call him by his first name, I met leaders whose gifts for ministry and passion for souls were unlike any I had met in the Episcopal world back home.

There were men like John Collins and John Lefroy, profoundly dedicated clergy who left spiritual legacies wherever they went. There was J. I Packer who, while not especially close to John Stott personally, nevertheless together with him brought Anglican evangelicalism into the mainstream of the global Christian community through his astute theological writings and practical pastoral wisdom. Both Packer and Stott became my *de facto* mentors, and it was to them that I dedicated my second book, written during the period when I served a parish in Toronto, *A Church To Believe In.*

There was also Michael Green, a pugnacious evangelist and gifted scholar with whom I was privileged to interact on many occasions over the coming years. Dick Lucas, the future Rector of Great St. Helen's Church in the City of London, was another luminary whom I came to know. He had a gift for expounding Scripture in an unforgettably exciting way, and parlayed that gift into a worldwide ministry of teaching others how to preach. In his dry, almost caustic manner, Dick could make you see something surprising in a familiar Bible passage and send you back to it with renewed curiosity and eagerness. Above all others, he became my model for biblical exposition. In addition to these men of God, there was Bishop David Sheppard, Bishop Maurice Wood, Bishop Stuart Blanche (later to become

Archbishop of York), and many other noted clergy whom I came to know through the wide door John Stott opened up to me.

BASH

But it was above all Bash himself whom I remember. On the surface the Rev. Eric Nash appeared to be a quintessential eccentric English bachelor. He dressed modestly and spoke carefully. He could slip almost unnoticed in and out of England's famous boarding schools in his handsome Rover with its walnut dashboard (a car that was a generous gift I later learned). He loved cucumber sandwiches served on Hovis bread. When he would appear on the Oxford or Cambridge campus, as he did at least once a term, young men would vie for the chance to serve him tea in their rooms. In his own quiet but powerful way Bash exercised an enormous influence on all who were around him.

I was never particularly close to Bash, in part because I think he was suspicious of all things American, and I sensed that. However, it was perhaps all things non-English? I did, however, on one occasion serve him the obligatory brown bread and cucumber sandwich in my rooms at Jesus College. Despite my lack of closeness, he became my model. I could see the impact he had on those around him, and observed the effective manner in which he translated spiritual passion into an enormously effective instrument for reaching the future leaders of England.

The camps he held during vacations took place in a lesser-known boy's boarding school in the South of England. They were a cover for a far more extensive outreach that included establishing Christian cells in schools like Eton, Harrow, Rugby, Repton, Wellington, Charterhouse, Haileybury, Monkton Coombe, Shrewsbury,

Marlborough and the like. It was in these historic schools that a mild and ritualized form of Christianity, as expressed in chapel and religion courses, actually inoculated most students from the real thing. Bash's aim was to win the ultimate loyalty of these boys and young men to Christ, and then send many of them back as teachers and eventually housemasters into the very schools from which they had come. Sometimes he worked with the cooperation of the school authorities, but at other times he worked under their suspicious eye and occasionally even with their outright disapproval. But his methods were impeccable, his personal lifestyle was above reproach, and the fruit of his work spoke for itself. John Stott was his most noted convert. Later I saw in print that no single individual had more to do with the shape of English Christianity in the second half of the twentieth century than Eric Nash.

Seeing the Bash camps in operation, camps that had been going for decades by the time I encountered them, only whetted my appetite for a similar ministry in the United States. Since, according to Peter Haile, I was a "typical Bash camper," it seemed natural for me to begin thinking about starting such a ministry once I returned home. But so much else had to happen first. For example, I first needed to get my degree from Oxford.

CHAPTER 7

OXFORD

THEOLOGICAL STUDY

Oxford proved a challenging academic experience but a far more enjoyable experience than my years at Yale. For one thing, I was no longer one of the most noticeable Christians on campus. Oxford in the late 1950s seemed to be a hotbed of Christian activity. Whereas at Yale only a handful of students would venture out on a Sunday morning to attend church, at Oxford as well as at Cambridge, I would estimate that as many as 60% or more would regularly attend the church of their choice.

Oxford offered a dizzying array of expressions of Christianity. As far as church was concerned, every brand of Christianity had its local institution and/or showcase parish—all within easy walking distance of the heart of the University. There was the "seriously evangelical" St. Ebbe's, packed to the gills with students eager to hear solid Bible-based sermons week after week from its redoubtable rector, Basil Gough. I made my home there. Then there was nearby St. Aldate's, a more open evangelical Anglican parish, also filled to the brim with students and visitors. A stream of bishops and other evangelical luminaries trooped through St. Aldate's, to the delight of the sermon tasters in the congregation. Later, when the charismatic movement was in full swing, St. Aldate's became known as the "charismatic parish" in town. A bit further along the High Street, you would find St. Mary the Virgin, the University Church, where broad-church preachers held forth on the virtues of a moral life, and the dangers of narrow-mindedness. St. Mary Magdalene was just up the road in St. Giles. There, those who wanted to be engulfed in incense, and hear the sound of bells signifying the precise moment when the bread and wine were transformed into the body and blood of Christ, would be welcomed. In addition there was Pusey House, an Anglo-Catholic center with a frigid but very comprehensive library. I often went there in search of peace and quiet in order to do serious study. In the winter I had to wear gloves inside, to keep my hands from going numb. In addition, there were many non-Anglican churches, plus a couple of dozen college chapels. Each residential college sported its own chapel with a full roster of services, a chaplain, and students who preferred to attend church in-college rather than to venture out to one of the many local parish churches. Sunday mornings in Oxford were rung in by a carillon of bells pealing from innumerable steeples. If you had looked forward to a comfy sleep-in after a long night at the local pub, you would be awakened with a start.

But the weekly event that I remember best was the Saturday night O.I.C.C.U. Bible "reading." O.I.C.C.U., pronounced "oy-kew," was the Oxford Inter-Collegiate Christian Union, the local expression on campus of the Inter-Varsity Fellowship. This movement had been formed in 1910 when Norman Grubb, an undergraduate at Cambridge, put this question to the leaders of the Student Christian Movement: "Do you acknowledge the atoning death of Jesus Christ to be central to your theology and teaching?" The answer they gave Grubb, whom I came to know many years later, was that "We believe it, but it is not central to our teaching." That answer led to the historic split between the SCM and the IVF, and the two movements took their separate paths. SCM withered away, along with much of liberal Protestantism, though it lasted into the 1970s, with campus groups around the world. In general, it was supplanted by the IVCF and its many international affiliates. When I last checked, a small Canadian SCM sported a website with a picture of Jesus looking like Che Guevara, and a banner that reads: "Liberation." Also, of course, in addition to those two student organizations there now exists a host of other Christian campus organizations vying for recruits.

Because I was looking for some way to dig into the riches of the Bible and apply it to everyday life, the Saturday night O.I.C.C.U. Bible readings proved the answer. A couple of hundred undergraduates, only a few of whom were theological students like me, would pack the Northgate Hall to listen to a lengthy, stimulating exposition of the Bible. This was not exactly everyone's idea of an exciting Saturday night date. However, more than any other single vehicle, these in-depth talks exposed me to some of the finest Christian teaching in the nation. One of my secret wishes during those years was that one day I might become well known and proficient enough to be invited to do an O.I.C.C.U. weekend myself, including a Saturday night Bible reading. That was never to be. However, I was invited to speak at a large conference in Oxford many decades later, and also at several other large conferences in England over the years. So I got my wish, though indirectly.

STUDENT LIFE

It would be wrong for me to give the impression that my time in England was all about attending Christian meetings, although as a young theological student I was playing spiritual catch-up with my

British brothers and sisters. I felt that they were much further along the Christian way than I. But, in addition to attending our Christian meetings, I enjoyed playing tennis for the Jesus College team. The gentlemanly approach to sport common in England in those days led to some amusing situations at intercollegiate meets. It was a sharp contrast with our typical American competitiveness. Tennis matches were played on the College's grass courts. Mid-way though the meet, all players would leave the court for afternoon tea (and cakes, of course). Tea was served in the College's sports pavilion. With a full stomach, all would proceed back onto the courts for more play. How we managed to keep going, I'll never know. I also recall attending the Henley Regatta, a splendid flag-flying, champagne and strawberry affair on a stretch of the Thames that rolled past a particularly bucolic part of England. Sport was a decidedly gentlemanly affair in England.

Speaking of food, which one must if one is writing of England in the decades after World War II, the quality was almost universally poor. Apart from sumptuous Sunday dinners, replete with roast beef, Yorkshire pudding, creamed cauliflower, lima beans, and perhaps a trifle or a treacle tart, the food was starchy, tasteless, fattening, and lacking in nutrition. Of particular memory were green peas floating in bright green water, salad cream—a murky yellowish cream that appeared on almost anything leafy—and fried bread. This was a breakfast staple so filled with fat that the grease virtually dripped off the bread. Lacking in nutritious food, I filled my stomach with crumpets (a unique version of English muffins), biscuits (i.e. cookies), and candy. Incidentally, I discovered that the English eat twice as much candy as Americans, and that the tax on all that candy just about covers the cost of the poor dental care provided through Britain's national health system.

By the end of my first semester at Oxford I had difficulty recognizing myself in the mirror, and so embarked on a serious diet. But I discovered that living on a student income, rarely spending more than a few shillings per meal, I was unable to guarantee anything close to a balanced diet. I did jog around the University Parks in an attempt to stay fit.

Because the National Health system was free, I decided to take advantage of it but with less than positive results. My American dentist had recommended the removal of my lower wisdom teeth. I went to a local hospital for this procedure. (In England one never goes to "the" hospital or stays in "a" hospital. One goes *to* hospital, and stays *in* hospital.) In any event, I have reason to believe that my dental surgeon was a novice. Not only was my throat very sore from the instrument he jammed down it to keep me from swallowing my tongue, but the nurse so badly twisted my ear in her effort to get me to wake up from the anesthesia that it was sore for days. Then, two weeks after the operation, while I was eating in a London restaurant, blood began to trickle down my chin. It was a hemorrhage due to the inadequate suturing job and I had to dash, pre-dawn, to a local emergency room for a hasty restitching job.

I managed to explore as much of the beautiful English countryside as I could, sometimes by myself, sometimes with others. Blenheim Palace, in nearby Woodstock, rewarded tourists like me who loved to tour historic homes and palaces. Eventually, I took my scooter to France and indulged a youthful passion to see the châteaux of the Loire. Posters of these magnificent royal estates had hung on my prep school walls, feeding a romantic vision as well as a lifelong love of architecture. When I finally got to the region, however, I was disappointed. The old tourist truism actually rang true: "You've seen one, you've seen 'em all."

During one vacation I drove north to the Lake District to attend the famous Keswick Convention, and on another to Scotland to participate in a beach mission to children. I hiked in the Yorkshire Dales and explored the Peaks District.

ACADEMIC CHALLENGES

Academically, Oxford presented some new challenges. Most of the learning in those days took place in libraries (as it still does) where students are expected to closet themselves away doing "research" and writing papers to be read out loud to a tutor. Lectures tend to be more or less optional. My theological tutor in Jesus College was Dennis Whiteley, a very peculiar man with strange mannerisms and a decidedly modernist approach to the Bible. I am sure that he hoped to liberalize my theological outlook, and only when he discovered that he could not do so, did he grow hostile. In fact, one day he virtually threw a fit in his study as I tried to navigate my way through the troublesome issue of criticism of the Pentateuch—that is, questions about the precise authorship of the first five books of the Old Testament. Unfortunately, Dr. Whiteley eventually became quite senile, and had to be let go. I fear he considered me one of the failures he brought with him to his grave.

Jesus was known as "The Welshman's College" because so many young students from Wales sought admission to the University through it. The name, familiar to English people, still sounded rather strange to my ears, especially when I heard crowds along the Isis (as the Thames is known in Oxford) screaming "Jesus, Jesus" as our College boat slithered through the waters at a regatta. But I met some fine men in that all-male environment, only a small number of whom were studying theology. It was not unusual to be stopped while walking around Oxford by a group of American tourists who wanted a picture of a "real Oxford student" in his academic gown. Imagine the surprise their faces registered when they discovered I was actually a homegrown boy from suburban New York!

My college rooms overlooked a back street that housed a couple of bars where motorcyclists would congregate until midnight. One night, totally fed up with the racket they created as they exited their favorite pub, I filled a waste basket with water, and emptied its contents three stories down on top of the motorcycles and their inebriated drivers. By the time they discovered the source of the splash of cold water on their faces, I had discreetly closed my window and retreated into the shadows!

I met and got to know many overseas students. One was Dick Bush, an Episcopal ordinand from Memphis who had already finished his theological degree at Yale Divinity School. Dick was a pensive guy, with a great gift for listening, and a capacity for deep friendship. He and I spent a lot of time together. Like most Episcopalians, Dick's only exposure to evangelical theology was through the distorted lens of Protestant liberalism. It was my joy to introduce him to some of the great English preachers like John Stott and Martin Lloyd-Jones. Lloyd-Jones, like Stott, had a huge congregation in London at Westminster Chapel just around the corner from Buckingham Palace. Dick and I found a common ground in our joint commitment to Christ, even though on some issues we were not on the same page. There were other expatriates whom we included in our circle. They were as diverse as Pete Dawkins, the noted West Point football player who was a Rhodes Scholar and a campus luminary, and Gilbert Gragg, an emotionally troubled Southerner. Gilbert was sure that Maggie Peale (daughter of the famous Norman Vincent Peale, author of *The Power Of Positive Thinking*) would succumb to his romantic overtures. However, she wisely married someone else.

L'ABRI

One could not be in England for two full years without trying to get to the Continent as often as possible. Over in Switzerland, on an alpine hillside just up from Montreux, an American Presbyterian minister named Francis Schaeffer had established L'Abri—a community for wandering students who were confused by the various secular philosophies that rivaled Christianity. L'Abri had already gained some notoriety through an article in *TIME* Magazine, and I was determined to check it out. So, on Christmas day in 1959, I bid goodbye to the small breakfast party at 12 Weymouth Street, at which John Stott and I had engaged in a water pistol fight around the dining room table, and headed off to Dover and the Channel ferry to France. I recall it as a particularly gloomy day, and I was feeling sorry for myself, alone and mindful of happy Christmases of the past. From Calais I proceeded by train to Switzerland where I spent a week trying to understand Francis Schaeffer and his approach to apologetics—the art of defending faith from its detractors.

Schaeffer appealed to me because he sought to relate biblical faith to a wide variety of cultural and intellectual issues. Although his knowledge of art, philosophy, and theology was incisive, it was usually thin. However, he excelled at portraying the dead end of secular thought, and the alternative provided by biblical faith. Students would drift in to his complex of mountain chalets from around the world, some seeking to escape the confines of narrow parochial thinking back home, others willing to give Schaeffer and his biblical worldview a try.

There was one side of Schaeffer's thought that troubled me. That was his ecclesiastical separatism. As a veteran of the Fundamentalist/ Modernist controversies of the early 20th. century, he was more aware than some of the great divide between these two schools of thought. He thought that the only way to be a faithful Christian was to abandon those denominations that had been infected with liberal theology and join new denominations like his brand of Presbyterianism. Because I was fired up with the vision of renewing the evangelical witness within the American Episcopal Church, this side of Schaeffer's thought left me unimpressed. Later, however, Dr. Schaeffer and his wife Edith came to admire the work that Sandra and I were doing through FOCUS, and we in turn sent many of our students to L'Abri for further deepening of their faith.

THE HOLY LAND

Two very special trips away from England during those memorable years at Oxford remain vital in my memory. One was a summer trip in 1959 to the Holy Land. My aunt Peggy had wanted to join me on the trip but at the last minute decided not to. However, she very generously sent me the money so that I could go. Traveling as cheaply as possible, I booked myself on a student train to Athens, and can still smell the non-working toilet that was just a yard from my face. The overcrowded train afforded me only that small space on the floor! Athens proved unbearably hot, with July temperatures hovering around 112 Fahrenheit. So, as soon as I could, I hopped a boat to Aegina, a Greek island frequented by local tourists in search of beaches and cool water. There I cooled off in the quiet waters of the Aegean.

Heading back to Athens, I then caught a flight to Israel. As I stepped off the plane in Tel Aviv I heard something unforgettable. I am not sure what I was expecting to hear during those first moments on the soil that had become so real to me from church and my study of the Bible. But the very first thing I heard was the comment of a young Israeli man to a friend. He said: "I don't have to pray to be a Jew." Well, of course not, I thought at the time. But his comment got me thinking: What really is a Jew? If what binds Jews the world over together is not the covenant with Abraham, Moses, and David, then what is it? Zionists would claim that it is a commitment to the nation of Israel as a homeland for world Jewry. Although I strongly supported the creation of Israel as a response of the Western democracies to the horrors of the Holocaust, I felt that this was an inadequate definition. If neither politics nor religion was the glue that held Jews together, what was? Ethnicity? Ethnically, Jews vary widely, with few identifiable characteristics that one could say were quintessentially Jewish. Not surprisingly, the question of "What is a Jew?" continues to bedevil scholars, including many Jewish scholars.

My trip to the Holy Land began with a visit to a synagogue. Two secular American Jewish lads were also eager to experience worship in the Holy Land. So we quietly snuck into a synagogue in Tel Aviv on Shabbat. I tried my best to hide my camera so as not to be seen as a tourist, sat between the two Jewish guys, and slunk down in my chair. But when, midway through the service, an elder approached me and asked if I would like to read from the Torah in Hebrew my cover was blown! With a polite smile, the rabbi chose another unsuspecting visitor.

Later, I rented a motor scooter and headed north to the region of Galilee. On my way I made the mistake of picking up a female hitchhiker. As she was in military uniform, I thought it would not be imprudent to offer her a ride. But only a half hour into our ride, out of the blue, she proposed marriage. Obviously, her proposal had nothing to do with romance, but everything to do with obtaining a Green Card in America. In retrospect, the whole incident seems funny.

Eventually I arrived at the headwaters of the Jordan, slightly north of the kibbutz at Dan. Unthinkingly, I crossed the narrow river on a little footbridge and began walking in an open field in the direction of nearby Mt. Hermon. But something made me feel uneasy about the dark shapes I could make out on a hill ahead of me. Making a hasty retreat I discovered that I had wandered across the border into Syria and could easily have been shot dead. I had a similar uneasy feeling when I crossed from the Israeli section of Jerusalem to the Jordanian side, the City being partitioned in that period. As I walked the "No Man's Land" that separated the two uneasy neighbors, soldiers with machine guns glared down at me from various pinnacles. It was a sobering reminder that being an American citizen does not protect one from any and every catastrophe.

Another memory of my only trip to the Holy Land was of a taxi ride in the Jordanian section of Palestine—now referred to as the West Bank. The car was filled with Arabs, one of whom turned around and glared at me wildly. "Have you been over there—to Israel?" he asked. I said yes. "You love Jewish men?" he demanded of me with a degree of venom I had only read about. "Well, I like them as well as I like anybody," I said. That didn't satisfy my fellow passengers, and a lively conversation ensued. Then one of the other Jordanian men turned to me and said: "You come and stay with me in my house for a year as my guest, and see Arab life close up." Because he had extended the invitation publicly and seriously, the man would have to be as good as his word. Of course, I declined. But I left this little interchange with a new appreciation of the stresses and strains of Jewish/Muslim relations in that troubled part of the world.

Actually, the first taxi ride I took, from Tel Aviv up to Jerusalem, was memorable too. I say "up" because the winding road ascends several thousand feet before it levels off on the plateau where the holy city sits. It happened to be a Friday afternoon, and our taxi was filled with businessmen hurrying home for the weekend. But something was bothering the taxi driver. He kept nervously looking back through the rear window at the setting sun, and his driving was erratic and hasty. It was as if he had a deadline to meet. And of course he did. The Sabbath, which officially begins at sundown Friday, was quickly approaching. If he—an observant Jew—were "working" at that time, he would be breaking the Law of God. I was impressed by his careful attention to duty, but also grateful for what Martin Luther called "the freedom of a Christian man."

THE CASBAH

My other major trip to the Continent was a spring vacation trip with my Dad and stepmother, Betsy. The two had married a couple of years after Mom and Dad divorced. Betsy, whose husband had died, was actually an old childhood friend of Dad's. This was a sort of belated wedding trip for the two of them. Our journey began in Portugal and went on to Madrid and southern Spain. The Spanish driver, who incessantly pointed out the remnants of Spain's Moorish past in the form of decrepit walls, turned out to be a fount of knowledge as well as a pretty good driver. We saw Goyas in Madrid, and toured the Alhambra in Granada.

We even made a brief side trip to Morocco. There, I took a quiet walk on the beach but had to escape the ever-present Arab boys eager for me to buy their "feelthy pictures." We dined in the Kasbah and enjoyed a demonstration by a nimble belly-dancer. But after dinner Dad remarked: "You did recognize that the dancer dressed in a long skirt with a bare midriff was actually a boy, didn't you?" I hadn't noticed.

With a driver, we motored deep into the Rift mountains, arriving at a colorful village where a young tour guide waited to escort us. "Are you Americans?" were the first words out of his mouth. "Yes," I replied. "Are you Christians?" "Yes." "Are you Protestants?" This was getting interesting. "Yes," I replied once more. "That is wonderful," he said. "We have two English missionary ladies living here who teach us the Bible," he said, displaying genuine excitement. As we walked through the town, I had a chance to draw him aside and ask, "Are *you* a Christian?" He looked quite surprised, and then with just a tinge of sadness, it seemed, said "No, I am a Muslim." "But why," I pressed. "You seem so interested in the Bible?" What he next said spoke volumes: "My father is a Muslim." That seemed to settle it. In Morocco, as in other Islamic countries, family and clan determine identity. There is almost no freedom to change one's religion.

My final semester at Oxford led up to the inevitable "D-Day" of final examinations. Working towards a degree, I had to do what every other student did: prepare with great vigor. In the "Oxbridge" system, everything depends on these exams. No work done prior to them counts. So for four months I prepared diligently. Together with nine of my friends, who shared a similar theological outlook, I reviewed the exams from previous years. Thankfully, they were all printed and available on the shelves of the Bodleian Library. Working as a team, we parceled out recurring essay questions and then wrote outlines of what we thought would be good answers on 3 by 5 inch, lined file cards. We even used mnemonic devices to help remember the key words or points. Over spring break that final year, and throughout our last semester, we would each borrow a few cards at a time and use them for review. It worked wonders. All of us did well on our exams, and got respectable grades. I recall my tutor, Dennis Whiteley, being quite surprised at my solid second.

For my final summer in England I headed for Cambridge to work on an extensive paper on the authority and inspiration of Scripture. Why? My studies had made clear that, as a conservative Christian working in a largely liberal denomination, I would have to learn to defend my position. If I made theological judgments, or argued specific Christian claims, I needed solid ground on which to stand. So, with the encouragement of J.I. Packer, whose then quite recent book, *Fundamentalism and the Word of God,* laid the issues out quite well, I chose to go to Tyndale House, an evangelical research library on the edge of Cambridge University.

There I began a hefty regimen of reading and writing. Was the Bible historically accurate? Was it infallible? Was in inerrant? Which scholars had a firm grasp of the truth? Who could I trust, given the fact that a virtual underground war between supernaturalists and anti-supernaturalists had been raging for at least a century. I read works on all sides of the issue, and hammered out a conclusion that I knew would not be popular with the teachers I would meet back in the States, as well as most clergy I would encounter afterward. By the end of the summer I was experiencing a fair amount of anxiety as I pondered returning to a denomination and its most liberal seminary. I later learned that I had reason to be wary.

Cambridge offered other rewards during those lazy summer days. There were teas at the famous Orchard in Grantchester, well known to many prominent English politicians and literati, tennis with young Englishmen sporting last names like Boddington, Collett-White, and Massingbird-Monday, and weekend jaunts to wonderful backwaters like Yorkshire's West Riding.

CHAPTER 8

VOCATION

REENTRY AND ORDINATION

Ultimately I had to face the question I had been putting off: should I be ordained? Given that my goal was to replicate the "Bash camps" in America, I questioned whether ordination would aid that task or hinder it. I also wondered if the Episcopal Church would be a good place for someone of my conservative and evangelical theological orientation.

My interview in England with visiting Professor Owen Thomas of the Episcopal Theological School of Cambridge, Massachusetts had much impressed me. "I see that you have been associated with Inter-Varsity Christian Fellowship at Yale," he quizzed. "At E.T.S. we would like to know if your views of the Bible have changed as a result of your studies at Oxford." I sensed it was a trick question. "Well, not especially," I admitted. "Then we at E.T.S. would like to know if you would be willing to submit your views on the Bible to radical re-evaluation if you come to study with us." "Of course I will," I said. "But while I re-evaluate them I'll continue to believe as I always have. I won't put my brain in a state of suspended animation." Later, a classmate at E.T.S., who happened to be on the Admissions Committee, told me that that my answer had nearly cost me a place.

Being uncertain about ordination, I prayed long and hard about it. But when the day came that I had to write a letter to the Bishop of Pittsburgh, with whom I had been corresponding, I sensed a freedom to move forward. That didn't stop me putting out a fleece: "Lord, I've got to make this choice; but would you give me a sign that the choice is the right one?" That morning I wrote the letter asking for ordination. As I went to bed that night, I realized that on that very day I had received letters from three clergymen in America. They all encouraged me to be ordained. I had my sign.

But an increasingly disintegrating family life awaited me back home. In fact, I wondered where *was* home? Facing questions like that, I decided that the comfort of food would help. So I bought a ticket on the *Liberté*, a French Line steamer, as my means of transport. Even in third class, I could count on the food being exceptional. However, once on board, overindulgence, lack of exercise, and the churning of the ocean turned my culinary adventure into an intestinal nightmare.

Nevertheless, I was beginning to see the hand of God in the little things. As I got on the tender in Southampton, I recognized a familiar face in the crowd. The name finally came to me: it was David Adeney. Adeney, an Englishman married to an American, had been a missionary to China. He had spoken to the Yale Christian Fellowship A couple of times during my time in New Haven. At the time he had impressed me as a man of wisdom and courage; he had returned to an unstable political situation in China on one occasion sick with malaria. And there he was on the same boat as me. When we met and exchanged stories, it was apparent to me that God had brought us together on this transatlantic crossing for my benefit. He was the perfect person to help me prepare for the challenges to come. This was a lesson in grace and wisdom I was never to forget.

EPISCOPAL THEOLOGICAL SCHOOL

I needed one more year of theology to qualify for ordination. In those days, E.T.S., where I enrolled, prided itself on being the most liberal theological seminary in the Episcopal Church. I had chosen it intentionally. I needed to learn to face the ideological and theological fire I knew would lie ahead. It didn't take long for that fire to flare up.

One of my first tasks was to take an English Bible exam. The seminary set this exam to determine whether incoming students knew anything about the Bible. It was an easy exam for me. My Oxford training had heavily emphasized biblical studies, and I had read the Bible personally for nearly a decade. We were told that only the names of those who passed the exam would be posted on the School's notice board.

When the day came, new students crowded around to see if their names were there. Mine was not. "What about Moore?" I could hear one or two of them saying. Despite my inquiries, it was several days before the professor responsible for the exam spotted me in a hallway. "Oh, Mr. Moore", he said. "We never looked at your exam. With your prior studies, you shouldn't have had to take it." I have always wondered if that was the true explanation.

This same professor chose another occasion to shame me in chapel in front of the senior class. He interrupted a sermon I was giving: "Mr. Moore, when are you going to sit down and let another student have a chance to speak?" He made clear that his objection was not just the length of the sermon, but disapproval over the way I was handling the text from the Gospel of John. There were other, similar events.

But that challenging year offered some very real compensations. A couple of professors quietly encouraged me. One, Dr. Albright, asked me to review the galleys of his biography of Phillips Brooks.

Another, Henry Shires, shared my Protestant leanings, and said so. But the one incident that stands out most clearly in my memory occurred right after that shaming in chapel. I sat down, red-faced, and ashamed. Soon the homiletics class was over. A student I slightly knew came up to me and asked: "What was all that about?" Either he could not understand the theological tension between my views and those of that professor (and most of the faculty), or he chose to act as if he didn't. "Where's your next class?" he asked. He then said, "Hey, I'm headed that way, too." I will never forget the show of quiet support expressed by that simple walk together across campus to my next class.

I did well academically. I graduated from E.T.S. "cum laude" and was told, with some apology, that the School did not have a "summa cum laude" to offer me. However, the reality was that the academic standards of Episcopal seminaries in those days were not all they were cracked up to be. Clearly we had a problem. There was both a lack of theological rigor and an almost pathological fear of anything orthodox, Scriptural, or evangelical. This was a perfect recipe for denominational drift.

One professor, Joseph Fletcher, seemed abnormally hostile toward anything orthodox. He viciously ridiculed one poor student who openly admitted that he believed in hell. Fletcher was soon to write a best-seller, *Situation Ethics*. Hailed as a major breakthrough among the quiche and Volvo set, the book managed to reduce all ethical decisions to one simple rule: "Whatever is done out of love is right." To the uninstructed reader, of course, this legitimized adultery, fornication, murder, homosexuality, and a host of other traditionally sinful activities, as long as the motive could be construed as love. College students devoured it. Fletcher managed to trash centuries of finely tuned ethical thinking, and erect his moral theory on a thoroughly subjective foundation. I wasn't surprised when a few years later Fletcher left the E.T.S. faculty and abandoned his ordination vows. He became a Humanist and signed the *Humanist Manifesto II* in 1973.

My mother had by now sold the Scarsdale house and retreated to "the wilds" of New Hampshire. Her hair in braids, she took to country life as an escape from everything familiar and suburban. She even romanticized her new location, Canaan, and for a while thought of herself as the "Bride" of Christ. Fortunately, either out of loneliness or from more serious reflection, she later quietly abandoned such cultish views and began to settle into a new and fairly normal life in northern New England.

I would visit her there in the three successive houses where she lived: first a lake house, then a farmhouse that tenants later burned to the ground, and finally a red Cape Cod-style house with a magnificent view of the Canaan valley and Mt. Cardigan that she and a very young builder constructed together. Never at a loss for things to do and abounding with energy, Mom gardened, got involved in local committees, made new friends, and continued to play tennis. In her early sixties she even defeated an eighteen-year old for the women's singles championship of New Hampshire. This earned her the admiration of a whole new circle of people. They, among others, persuaded her to run for the New Hampshire House of Representatives. She ran, but lost to a man.

I don't want to imply that my mother's somewhat strange theological views were entirely moderated over time. She and I still had what some have called "vigorous fellowship" over issues surrounding the end times. But in New Hampshire she kept these views largely to herself. She even took up smoking an occasional cigarette and having wine with dinner—habits that on the surface did not jibe with her rather strange views. These habits did, however, make her seem a bit more approachable to others.

Eventually, Mom reconciled with her mother and father, and made several trips back to Scarsdale to visit them. It was on one of these visits that Nana looked at Mom and then me and asked, "Now tell me, when did you two first meet?" The dementia that she was beginning to evidence was, unfortunately, later to afflict my mother too.

Upon reflection, I was saddened that my mother's worldview did not seem to include grace—God's unconditional, and unearned acceptance of us sinners because of the cross of Christ. Her worldview was one of right and wrong, judgment and fear. Nor did she ever really experience the benefit of a local group of Christians with whom she could share the pain and joy of life. Perhaps if she had, their honest love might have helped smooth out some of the rough edges of her character. She did go, on occasion, to events sponsored by the Worldwide Church of God—a cult spawned by a broad radio ministry and flashy magazine called *The Plain Truth*. But the give and take of peers who know you and love you despite your faults, one of the great treasures of being a part of a vital church, was not apparently available to her.

ORDINATION

I was ordained to the diaconate in June of 1961, and promptly went to serve as deacon-in-charge of a newly named mission, All Soul's Episcopal Church in East McKeesport, Pennsylvania. My connection with the Diocese of Pittsburgh, which proved vital to founding Trinity Episcopal School for Ministry much later, had begun with an association with Sam Shoemaker. "Sam", as everyone knew him, was the dynamic rector of Calvary Church in the Shady Side section of Pittsburgh. There he gained a wide reputation for preaching, writing, and evangelism. In his early years as Rector of another Calvary Church—this one on lower Park Avenue in Manhattan -- Sam had become involved with Frank Buchman, the founder of the Oxford Groups Movement that later became Moral Re-Armament. He also had a hand in helping create Alcoholics Anonymous, a truly life-saving ministry. In addition, Sam founded Faith-at-Work, a movement aimed at bringing lay people into an encounter with Jesus Christ. Preceded by what amounted to notoriety in elite circles, Sam would regularly visit college campuses, especially those of the Ivy League. On such occasions, he would spot eager, well-intentioned pagans among the students and arrange to meet with them one-on-one. It wouldn't be long before he popped the question: "Son, have you ever thought of the ministry?" The usual embarrassed response was "What? Who? Me?" The young man had typically never dreamed of such a radical step. "Well, what's preventing you?" Sam would ask.

That would invariably lead to frank confession of sin, which was just where Sam was headed, of course. The star-stricken undergraduate would soon be on his knees confessing his sins, and would leave dazed, wondering what had just happened. Some of Sam's converts stuck to their newfound faith. But many did not. The university chaplains who had invited Sam to their campus were aware of his evangelistic leanings (as well as his mesmeric effect on young men). But because his theology was experiential rather than biblical, they also knew that the fruit of his ministry would provide new recruits for their liberal theology once the romance of conversion wore off.

I became acquainted with Sam Shoemaker on one of his visits to Yale and before I left for Oxford. My good friend Larry McCullough and I attended a conference for young men considering the ministry that he sponsored in Pittsburgh. The Pennsylvania Turnpike had only been fully opened seven years earlier; but Larry and I drove all the way from New Haven to Pittsburgh for the event. Unimaginable in our day of rising costs of gasoline, in those halcyon days, gasoline hovered around 25 cents per gallon. I remember when once it even dipped to 19 cents.

Most of the young men at the conference had been touched by Sam Shoemaker's ministry on one of his campus visits. But very few of them had even a rudimentary grasp of the Gospel. They were fired with the same idealism that a generation later would cause many to become anti-war activists and to question all authority. But Sam fulfilled a crucial need. He was a voice calling for personal commitment to Christ, and to a life of service and ministry. His small book, *A Young Man's View of the Ministry,* is a classic.

Sam was always ready with a quip or a joke, especially when at the expense of his own denomination. I recall him telling me, with amusement, of the latest theological definition of "worship" to come from national Episcopal headquarters. "Worship is bi-polar liturgical action," said the document, solemnly. "Sounds like birth control to me," grunted Sam in his inimitable way.

Because the Bishop of Pittsburgh fast-tracked me for ordination in the June immediately following my graduation from E.T.S., I was soon kneeling before him for the laying on of hands for the diaconate, held at St. Paul's Church in Mt. Lebanon.

My family's reactions were characteristic. Nana had never flown in her life, and was never to fly again. But she made it to Pittsburgh, reminding me of how much I owed to the witness she provided to me and others of how a believer should approach the Bible. My father also came, but not my mother. Mom's great reservations about the church kept her from ever being fully reconciled to the fact that I was ordained. I can't recall her ever addressing a letter to me as "The Rev." Peter Moore. While she did approve of FOCUS when she saw the fruit of that ministry, she showed no interest in the ecclesiastical side of my life.

I originally expected to join Sam Shoemaker as a curate at Calvary Church in Pittsburgh. Coincidentally, my cousin Ted Beck had nearly taken that same position himself some years earlier. He had been touched by Sam's ministry at Princeton, attended Virginia Seminary, and spent a decade or so in the ordained ministry. But later he left the ministry and took up academic life. Unfortunately, many clergy who abandoned their youthful faith sadly remained in orders. This would lead to preaching that was more akin to agnosticism than biblical faith. Ted's decision I thought showed a certain intellectual honesty.

In the end, I could not serve as Sam's curate. Midway through my year at E.T.S., he abruptly resigned his rectorship under somewhat questionable circumstances and quietly retired to his family estate outside Baltimore. Over the succeeding years, I remained friendly with the Shoemakers even though I was privately relieved at the prospect of not having to live in Sam's shadow. His very forceful personality, masked by ebullience and bonhomie, always made me wonder if I could work effectively under his tutelage. His larger than life image proved too sharp a contrast to that of John Stott who, with his humility and scholarship, always remained my ideal model of ministry.

WET BEHIND THE EARS

As a result, for the next two years, I was in charge of All Soul's Parish in East McKeesport, in the dingy industrial suburbs east of Pittsburgh.

The town still wore the patina of decades of soot spewed into the air by the thriving steel industry. For me, it proved to be a trial by fire. "My, what a young man we have for a minister" one octogenarian commented at my welcoming reception. Of course, she was right. I knew precious little about parish life, and even less about leading worship. Moreover, I fitted into the social scene of the Mon Valley (the Monongahela River flowed nearby) like a fish out of water. With nary a thought about the implications, I purchased a second-hand MG sedan, made of foreign steel. My tough steel-mill parishioners let me know of their disapproval.

But this two-year parish posting offered the challenge of bringing people from nominal faith to real faith. I struggled with how to do this in an ecclesiastical environment that stresses tradition, ceremony, and liturgical correctness. Had these people ever been challenged with the offer of a serious personal commitment to Christ? Some proved responsive to my preaching.

I soon formed a Bible study group that met in the basement of the rectory and the group began to feel like a nucleus of something new and life-giving. We began to see God do remarkable things. One couple, completely outside the parish but related to one of our group members, was desperate financially. They were facing Christmas jobless, with no presents for their children. We gathered food and wrapped presents, and made sure that they had a Christmas. Soon Bill and Tina Rose were a part of our group, and the signs of genuine conversion were written all over their faces.

I also began a "Fall Teaching Mission." Passing out American Bible Society portions of the New Testament, I attempted to preach a series of sermons, expounding Galatians the first year, and Ephesians the second. I realized that the Word was getting through when one newcomer left church one Sunday saying: "I never thought of the

Bible that way." Soon she and her husband were regular members, and not long after I left the parish, the two volunteered as missionaries with another denomination.

I found that living as a single man in holy orders presented some surprising and awkward challenges. One member of the parish and his wife were particularly solicitous of me, almost from the moment of my arrival. They showered little presents on me, and volunteered for just about everything.

But then "payday" came. The husband asked, "Peter, will you do me a favor?" "Well, Bill," I said, "what is the favor?" "Just say you'll do me the favor." "I can't, Bill, until I know what it is." But by then I was so socially indebted to him and his wife that I felt I had to say, "OK." "Just ask Roberta to the circus," he said.

Well, Roberta was their unmarried daughter, in her late twenties and religious but not at all attractive in my eyes. She was already becoming seriously obese. But I was stuck, and so did the gentlemanly thing.

Next Sunday, Bill confronted me at the door of the fire hall where we were holding services (our old church had been sold, and our new one was not yet built): "Peter, everyone is talking." "Talking about what, Bill?" I asked. "You know. Talking about you and Roberta." "What?" I exclaimed, maybe sounding a little too surprised. "About me and Roberta? There's absolutely nothing between me and Roberta." I'm sure I made my case too strongly because from that point on, Bill and his wife ceased to take me into their confidence.

Another, even more embarrassing, experience happened when an unhappily married mother of three in the parish tried to lure me into her bedroom after a quiet lunch in her home. It was neither the first, nor the last, of such advances. But either out of fear, or I'd like to think a bit of self-control, with God's grace I managed to wait for marriage. But in those lax days, when fornication was almost an essential rite of passage for young men, it wasn't easy. Inevitably, feelings of inadequacy dogged my steps. My bishop, Bishop Pardue, didn't help much when he casually said to me: "Peter when it comes to sex, just do your best." I was never sure what he meant but it was probably intended as a word of grace at the time.

In those days, I used commercial buses whenever possible to save money. Later, I traveled by plane whenever possible, but not in the years when my salary was in the low four figures.

On one occasion I had gone to Philadelphia to do various things, including listen to Billy Graham at one of his crusades. Late that night, I took a bus back to Pittsburgh, asking the driver to drop me off in my hometown, East McKeesport, which was on his route. From the traffic light there, I could walk the one mile home, carrying my small suitcase. It would save me going all the way into the City and then coming back.

I took a sleeping pill so that I could get some sleep after a busy day, and dozed off. Half way across the Pennsylvania Turnpike the bus pulled into Midway, where there was a gas station and a restaurant. "Anyone wishing to use the facilities may do so now," said the driver. Half asleep, I dallied a few minutes, and then left my sports jacket and suitcase by my seat and sauntered into the bathroom.

I emerged a few minutes later, just in time to see my bus, my jacket, and my suitcase zoom off in a cloud of exhaust. Desperate, I began talking to anyone who might take me as far as they were going. Finally a man in a convertible (it was a warm summer night) offered, and we sped off into the darkness.

About an hour and a half later, he said to me, "There's your bus up ahead." The lights of a Greyhound appeared a couple of miles up ahead of us. We pulled up alongside the huge bus and, traveling at about 80 miles an hour, I gestured from the passenger side of the car to the bus driver that I belonged in *that* bus. He got the message and pulled over. I said goodbye to my convertible driver, and the bus door swung open. Only it was a strange driver. Not my bus at all.

The driver did not believe my story but it turned out that he was, fortunately for me, going to Pittsburgh and not bypassing Pittsburgh for Cleveland, as a number of buses did. Just as dawn broke, we exited the Turnpike and headed in on Route 30. At that point I noticed another Greyhound up ahead, and wondered if it might be *my* bus. Quite surprisingly, we caught up to that bus exactly at the point where I had requested a special stop so that I could get off. Sure enough, as we pulled up behind that bus, the light turned green, and the bus in front did not move. I got out of my bus, banged on the door of the bus ahead, jumped in, grabbed my jacket and suitcase, and walked home.

The whole story was such a testimony to God's ability to cover for my stupidity, that I wrote it up and sent it to *Reader's Digest* in the hopes that they might include it in their "Life in these United States"" column. But it never saw the light of day—until now.

THE EPISCOPAL CHURCH

The Episcopal Church was in its heyday in the early 1960s. In 1965 it had 3,615,000 baptized members. But every year thereafter it showed a decline. By 1970, for example, the number had decreased slightly to 3,475,000, while the population had grown. However, by 2001, with significant growth in the population, the total number of baptized members had dropped to 2,317,000 a decrease in 35 years of 1,300,000 souls. This remarkable decline was happening to most of the so-called mainline Protestant denominations in America. And the causes of the downward trend were evident.

Most Episcopal preaching was dull, formulaic, and uninspired. It lacked any ring of biblical authority. Preachers whose churches were located on the edges of struggling urban areas, in the inimitable words of Sam Shoemaker: "stroked fat congregations with the rewards of a virtuous life while great teeming masses of humanity only a short distance away struggled for a decent meal or a breath of clean air." Hypocrisy was writ large. A position on the vestry of an Episcopal Church, for example, was a step up socially for most. Manners, protocol, church furniture, finery, and processions, plus worldly deference to courtly bishops gave the church an air of pomp and self-importance that was as far removed from the dynamism of the early church in the Book of Acts as one could get. Few clergy knew or even preached the Gospel that we are all sinners and can only hope for salvation through the gracious work of Christ on our behalf on the cross.

Although written unmistakably into our liturgy, thanks to forebears who knew their Bibles and even paid for their faith with their lives, the Gospel as such was lost in the majestic cadences of Elizabethan English and Gregorian chants. Episcopalians were defined by who they were not—not Baptists, not Fundamentalists, not schismatics, not "congregationalist," not holy rollers, not Roman Catholics, not pietists—the list could go on. The Episcopal Church had an air of sanctity but made very few demands on personal behavior. Financial giving was exceptionally poor. Knowledge of the Bible was almost non-existent. Being Episcopalian was as much a social statement as a religious one.

Episcopalians, for the most part, laughed at the idea of evangelism. Despite the Church of England's warm reception of Billy Graham

Episcopal clergy had little time for anything smacking of crusades. It is hard to avoid the verdict that Jesus pronounced on the Pharisees of his day: "They had the form of religion, while denying its power."

However, the seeds of awakening existed, and many lifelong Episcopalians, unknown to themselves, had internalized Christian doctrine without actually professing it thoughtfully. It was inevitable that this benign hypocrisy could not go on forever. As the culture of the 1960s began to veer sharply away from traditional mores, all hell would begin to break loose.

CHAPTER 9

NEW YORK YEARS

FOCUS IS BORN

As I mentioned earlier, from the moment of my return to the States from England, I had cherished within my heart a desire to establish a ministry similar to the Bash camps of England. In fact, I had already begun it while in seminary. Much of the story is told in *Be Thou Our Vision* by Molly O'Donovan and Brooke Gunning, published on the 25th anniversary of the founding of FOCUS. But parts of it are worth recounting here.

In the winter of 1961, a group gathered at my invitation in New Hampshire for what turned out to be a very snowy weekend. In fact it was a minor blizzard. One of the participants was Bill Wasch, who was married to my cousin Susan Beck Wasch. Both had had their faith renewed through the Billy Graham Crusades. Bill's car battery had died but the heavy snow that fell all weekend made the long driveway that descended to the main road from the hillside where my mother's farmhouse stood impassible. In desperation, we loaded it onto a sled and trudged off to get it re-charged. Finally a plough came, so we could leave.

Without healthy fare from a supermarket, we cooked meals that weekend consisting of 95% starch. But it hardly mattered; we were reading prepared papers to each other on how a ministry to the private secondary schools of the Northeast might look. Could we work with the chaplains or must we go around them? How would we get a foot in the door? What kind of vacation events should we have? Where should they take place?

Meanwhile, I had built a relationship with Dr. Frank Gaebelein, the noted evangelical scholar and founding headmaster of Long Island's Stony Brook School. Dr. Frank happened at the time to be chair of the Board of a then 75-year old organization known as the Council for Religion in Independent Schools. C.R.I.S., as it was familiarly known, had grown out of the Christian student movements of the early 1900's—the same seedbed, actually, from which the modern ecumenical movement had emerged. Religious conferences for students from private boarding schools had been held as far back as the teens and twenties of the 20th century, and from those conferences this small organization, aimed at serving the religious needs of these schools, had been formed. The Council had no confession of faith around which to rally, and it included schools with a great diversity of denominational and non-sectarian affiliations: Episcopalian (of course), Quaker, Presbyterian, Methodist, Moravian, and so on. The Roman Catholic schools were not a part of the organization, as they presumably had their own.

THE COUNCIL

The home office of C.R.I.S. was located in what has often been called the "God Box"—the Interchurch Center erected adjacent to the famous Riverside Church in New York City. It was diagonal from

Union Theological Seminary and very close to Columbia University. Inside this imposing building at 475 Riverside Drive resided a wide range of ecumenical organizations. Upstairs, the National Council of Churches occupied several floors. C.R.I.S., by contrast, occupied two small rooms on the second floor.

The aim of C.R.I.S. was to assist chaplains and religion teachers in the independent schools through curriculum suggestions, conferences for faculty, triennial conventions for school heads, chaplaincy placement assistance, and most notably a series of student conferences held in major centers of independent schools. Typically the conference topics were "Christianity *and*..." or "Religion *and*...." You can put almost anything after that: politics, morality, your emotions, vocation, the War (the Viet Nam War was picking up steam as a major campus obsession), sex (a favorite), and so on. The speakers tended to be seminary professors, college religion teachers or chaplains, noted authors, accomplished laity, and even occasionally someone in government.

I asked Frank Gaebelein how I could somehow get a foot in the door of this organization, thinking that through the Council I might gain credibility and win access to some of the very schools that were on my radar. His answer surprised me: "Why don't you give some money to it?" That idea, of course, had been furthest from my thoughts. Nevertheless, I did send in $100 and received an effusive letter of thanks. Little did I know that this was precisely the way to get noticed. Imagine sitting in your small New York office, and a nobody clergyman from the wilds of Southwestern Pennsylvania up and donates $100. You want to know: "Who is this guy?" In a cash-strapped organization, an unsolicited donation was news.

I soon learned that there was a staff opening. Bill Swing, who was many years later to become Episcopal Bishop of California, was leaving. I applied, drove to New York, was interviewed, and was quickly hired as his replacement. The Council's then Director was Earl Harrison, a genuinely open-minded Friend—that is, he was a Quaker. Because the words "Episcopalian" and "evangelical" had almost no connection with each other in the minds of the board members who hired me, I was ushered into the inner sanctum of this small fraternity with little regard for my theological convictions. I don't recall one question being asked about what I believed or even of my motives in the interview.

I was in for a huge surprise on my first day of work. As I walked in the door that day in September of 1963, I met the woman who had been the power behind the throne of C.R.I.S. For more than two decades, Dorothy Palmer had held the tiny organization together with industry and vision. But her liberal Presbyterianism and my conservative Anglicanism were inevitably going to clash at some point. Thankfully, the clash never happened. Dorothy greeted me on my first day of work with the news that she had just resigned because, as she put it, "Earl had decided to stay this extra year." With those words, she not only told me that she was leaving, but implied that my boss would be gone in a year or less. Since the organization had only three staff members, I thought I saw the hand of God. Here was the opportunity to head the only national organization serving the religious needs of the private schools in America. It could be potentially mine at the tender age of 27. Nine months later I became Director of C.R.I.S.

RIVERSIDE DRIVE

To summarize my years from 1963 to 1973 briefly is hard to do. These years were filled with job-related travel, speaking opportunities, conferences, and administrative work. I lived in a very modest apartment at 139th street and Riverside Drive. It was a brand-new, state-aided, middle-income cooperative that I purchased for a mere $2,500. It even provided me with a coveted parking space for the astonishing price of $15 per month. It was strategically located, with ready access to Riverside Drive, on which I could zoom downtown or uptown to the George Washington Bridge. I could be in Westchester County on my way to New England in a flash. In short, it was the perfect bachelor pad.

I painted it white, and installed a midnight blue carpet, which I cared for compulsively, for which I was justifiably ribbed by friends, including John Yates who cited my compulsion in a toast at Sandra's and my wedding some five years later. With some really nice furniture I had inherited or bought, the place was very attractive, even though the neighborhood was not considered genteel. It featured a terrace covered with an imitation green grass carpet, on which were two director's chairs and a hibachi grill. Beyond the sliding glass doors and the terrace was a panoramic view of the Hudson River and the entire Manhattan skyline. A great many friends trooped through New York City seeking a place to sleep, and found solace there. Charlie Drew, later to become a noted pastor and author, even spent a summer there with me while interning with C.R.I.S. For a time, I had a roommate, Harvard graduate Bob Lee, who had secured a place as an alternate oarsman at the Tokyo Olympics and was taking courses at Union Seminary. But, given the job I had, I was away far more often than I was there. Across the hallway lived Don and Cola Peguese, a black couple who befriended me. I was on a first name basis with them until Don was tragically killed in a freak accident. Instantly, I once again became "Reverend Moore" to Cola, who needed me as a pastor more than as a friend.

A remarkable experience occurred there one Saturday afternoon. Unexpectedly my doorbell rang; and the visitor turned out to be my African-American next-door neighbor who was a detective with the New York Police Department. Dressed in a tuxedo with a flower in its buttonhole, he was obviously very worried. He told me that the priest who was to marry his daughter had failed to appear. However, it was too late to cancel, and all the guests had arrived. Out of the blue, he then asked me if I would perform the wedding then and there. I'm not sure whether it was providential but I forgot the rule that, as a clergyman, I am not permitted to perform weddings on less than 24 hours notice. However, this was the height of the Civil Rights movement, and my neighbors were facing a major crisis. Given those facts, I might well have gone ahead even if I had known.

I agreed, got dressed, and appeared in the adjacent apartment in a suit and clerical collar within 15 minutes. When I walked in, it looked to me as if the reception had already begun. A large crowd was gathered and sandwiches were arranged on platters on tables. I was the only white person there. Undaunted I walked into the bedroom where the bride was waiting in her wedding dress, and asked her if she was a member of a Christian church, and she affirmed that she was. I told her that there were a few other things she would need to say during the ceremony, to make the wedding official, and she agreed. Then I walked into the other bedroom where the groom was standing. He seemed less friendly than I would have expected, given the fact that I was doing him a real favor. Again, I was assured that he was a church member and I explained what would happen at the service. Then all of us walked into the crowded living room for the brief service. After it was over and I had pronounced them "man and wife", I retired to my apartment.

Two hours later the doorbell rang again. I opened it to find the groom standing by himself. "I have come to pay my debt," he said. "Oh, just keep your money to yourself," I said to him. "I just want you and your wife to have a happy and blessed marriage." "It will be happy and blessed," he said, with steely eyes, "because it will be lived under the Universal Spirit." "It will be lived under the Universal Spirit?" I said. "Are you a Christian?" I asked. "No," he said definitively. "Is your wife a Christian?" I asked. "No," again. "Are you a Black…" Then I quickly amended it to, "Are you a Muslim?" "Yes," he said. "Is your wife a Muslim?" "Yes," again. "Well, then, you've deceived me, haven't you?" I said. "You've gone against the dictates of your own religion."

The story has stayed with me, because it seemed so strange at the time. Recall, that this was the era of the so-called Black Muslims, and this incident occurred decades before the emergence of "radical Islam." Black Muslims, or The Nation of Islam, as this unique brand of African American Muslims call themselves, had grown up on American soil, believing among other things that the white man was the devil. The groom's response when I confronted him with his lie was: "We don't believe in living in sin." Sometime afterwards it occurred to me that he was living with a moral hierarchy: Lying to a white man was not nearly as wrong in his mind as living together out of wedlock. Given his views of white people, I can understand that. I asked him: "Will you please come back and talk about this with me some time?" He said yes; but we never saw each other again. I can only guess that the priest who was scheduled to do the wedding discovered the couple's religious faith, and at the last minute refused to show because of it.

STUDENT CONFERENCES

The board of the Council for Religion was composed of headmasters and chaplains from some of the nation's elite independent schools. All seemed to be well intentioned, but because the organization had no theological foundations despite the distinct Christian ring of its acronym, it was pluralist to the core. Each school defined religion as it wished. The Council existed to assist them all and to share ideas that would be helpful to them in their chapel programs and in the courses in religion and ethics that they offered. Frank Gaebelein was welcomed as Board Chair out of respect, and there were a few orthodox Episcopalian headmasters and Trinitarian Quakers. But the majority of those in the board's inner circle were typical liberal Protestants, and—if truth be told—deathly afraid of anything smacking of evangelical zeal.

I learned to play the game that such a unique situation required. At the large student conferences, there would be speakers of all persuasions. These conferences were held at a conference center outside of Concord, NH for northern New England schools, at the Inn at Buck Hill Falls, PA, for the middle Atlantic and NYC schools, in Virginia for the Southern schools, and at Gatlinburg, TN, for schools in the Deep South. I did my best to make sure that at least some of the speakers were committed Christians. However local committees chose speakers, and those chosen had to be wise enough to speak into our pluralistic situation with sensitivity. Ernest Gordon, the Dean of the Chapel at Princeton, who had written an account of his World War II experiences in *Miracle on the River Kwai*, was a favorite of mine, and it turned out of the students too. So was Armand Nicholi, the evangelical psychiatrist who taught at Harvard. I even got Dick Lucas, my preaching role model from England who was on tour in the States, to come and speak.

But interspersed with these occasional Christ-centered speakers were others whose "gospel" was a warmed over version of the anti-Viet Nam rhetoric of the day, and whose theology owed more to Modernism than to St. Paul. I ached for the hundreds of students each year that attended these conferences to hear the Gospel. But even though I headed the sponsoring organization, speakers were chosen by committees made up of chaplains who held a wide variety of views.

Because the Council flourished under my direction, I was able to operate more or less under cover. However, when one of the chaplains I knew whispered to a group of cronies (in my hearing), "Do you know that Peter Moore is a Fundamentalist?" the game was up. That word, even though misapplied in my case, was the kiss of death, and was probably meant to be. I realized it was time to seek an exit from C.R.I.S. Over successive years, C.R.I.S. changed its name to something dealing with "moral values" because its older name had too much of a Christian ring. Its conference ministry died out and, although something like C.R.I.S. still exists, it is a shell of its former self.

APOSTLE TO THE PREPPIES

Being head of the only national organization serving 300 independent secondary schools in the field of religion afforded me some remarkable experiences. Bob Moss, longtime headmaster of St. Andrew's School, Delaware, and Chair of the Board of the Council for most of the years while I was the Executive Director, wrote in his history of the Council: "Peter Moore was sensitive to the spiritual hunger of students in the midst of all the confusion that was taking place at schools." He was referring to the turbulent Sixties during which so many schools abandoned their distinctly Christian heritage. (I refer you to: *Voices Of Religion in Independent Schools, the Evolution of the Council For Religion in Independent Schools*, Robert A. Moss, 1993, p.64.)

My decade with the Council for Religion gave me valuable exposure to the entire independent school scene in the United States. I made hundreds of school visits in nearly every state during that time, and in most was given a warm welcome, and chance to teach a class, speak in chapel, address the entire student body in assembly, talk to the faculty, or in the case of a few, even to lead a "religious emphasis week." On one of these occasions, Robert Yardley, headmaster of Chatham Hall, dubbed me the "apostle to the preppies" and made me an honorary graduate of his school.

I had three opportunities to lead religious emphases weeks at Atlanta's Westminster Schools. One year I talked about the modern rivals to Christian faith, and turned the substance of those talks into my first book, *Disarming the Secular Gods*. It bore some similarity to a book that had been published a decade or more earlier, *Campus Gods On Trial* by Chad Walsh. I tried to analyze alternatives to Christian faith, showing their strengths and weaknesses. The talks would be followed by class after class peppering me with questions to which I gave the best answers I could. These sessions always seemed to reveal the bankruptcy of non-Christian worldviews, and sharpen my ability to make a case for the Faith. The book, published in 1989, doubled as my thesis in the Doctor of Ministry program I completed at Fuller Seminary and, to my surprise, won a Gold Medallion Award from the ECPA (Evangelical Christian Publishers Association) as the best book of the year in their evangelism category.

I also have a raft of humorous war stories from these years with C.R.I.S. There was the time a headmistress told me not to mention the name of Jesus in the talk I was about to give. I went right ahead and did so. There was another headmaster who less warmly-welcoming than most, issued a disclaimer just before my talk, saying that the school did not necessarily affirm what I was about to say and that, even though it was a required assembly, any student who wished to leave could now do so. And there was the time when, after I preached about the Resurrection of Christ on Easter Sunday, a delegation of faculty stormed into the headmaster's office saying that he was favoring one religion over another by inviting me to speak. That was Deerfield Academy, and I was never asked back. These incidents could be multiplied *ad nauseam;* and as I think back, I smile. What a small price to pay for the great privilege of speaking, as a convinced Christian, to a whole generation of bright high school students. I was supported by many who prayed for me, and was undergirded by the confidence that God had called me to this world of independent school students. Consequently, I was never discouraged. In fact, I was energized by the opposition I received.

One of the more humorous incidents during these years was the Sunday that Sandra joined me at Brooks School north of Boston. The chaplain had invited me to speak in chapel, somewhat nervously, I think. The Gospel's so-called "scandal of particularity"—that is, the claim that Jesus is *the* one and only Savior of the world—was a frightening concept to him. Like many chaplains, he feared a backlash from humanistic faculty, headmasters sensitive to non-Christian parents, and skeptical students. There was no desire to engage with the exclusive claims of Christ. I often thought that a tacit agreement existed between chaplains and the school heads that had hired them: no proselytizing! At any rate, that evening, during the question time following my chapel talk, the chaplain did his best to "reinterpret" what I was saying to the boys lest any student leave with the dangerous impression that Jesus might actually be the Way, the Truth, and the Life, as Jesus had claimed. "Would you like to have a cup of coffee," he asked Sandra, hoping to bring the evening to a speedy close. Completely attuned to the opportunity of the moment, Sandra quickly agreed: "A fine idea." He then took her arm and led her out of the room, leaving me alone with a roomful of boys eager to hear more. When he turned and realized that I was not following them, and that he was surrendering control of the meeting he had a stunned expression on his face. Sandra and I had many a laugh later at his expense.

The staff of C.R.I.S. was one of the real joys of this era of my life. Larry Miller, a Union Seminary graduate, and an ordained Presbyterian minister, had discovered the reality of Christ after seminary during a sojourn in Africa. He had all the right credentials, and a very pleasing personality as well, so the board was delighted when I hired him as my Associate Director. Heidi Frost, a close associate of Sam and Helen Shoemaker, who was later to work with Bruce at Faith at Work, an early renewal organization, was my Conference Coordinator. Heidi later married a judge in Texas, and found her niche in raising his children and theirs. Like Larry, Heidi was in effect an undercover evangelical at that point. With her winsome ways, she made friends everywhere. Laurel Franks, a Mt. Holyoke graduate from Canada, later replaced Heidi, and brought a deep conviction that God answers prayer to her work with C.R.I.S. Finally, Geoff Rawlins, who was ordained in the Church of England, came "across the Pond" to work with us in the area of what we called "junior" schools—or pre-prep schools. Geoff had matured while working under John Stott at All Souls. His artistic temperament and blue-blood credentials (not to say his impeccable British accent) ensured a warm welcome from parents and faculty.

Soon, the growing network of friends and supporters sensed that "something was happening" in the prep school world. Never before and never since, had the Council for Religion gathered such a large staff or had such a wide reach. Conferences burgeoned, contacts multiplied, doors opened, and the organization was involved in the life of many more schools than before.

THE RADICAL SIXTIES

Then came November 23, 1963, and the shot heard around the world—President Kennedy, assassinated by Lee Harvey Oswald, while riding in a motorcade in Dallas. The world came to a standstill and watched as a stunned and disbelieving nation mourned the murder of their young President. I was just outside of Concord, New Hampshire, at a C.R.I.S. conference for northern New England boarding schools when I heard the news. After the conference I retreated to Cambridge, Massachusetts, to stay with Joe and Grace Brown, who had been instrumental in the earliest years of FOCUS. Joe, was an instructor at Harvard at the time, while completing his Ph.D. Later he became an eminent conservative Protestant theologian and seminary professor. He and Grace were dear friends to me, and also to Sandra in the early years of our marriage. Sadly, Joe died a couple of years before I began this memoir.

President Kennedy's death added fuel to the fire of what came to be known as the radical Sixties. Anti-Viet Nam war rhetoric rose to a crescendo. Students burned their draft cards and/or emigrated to Canada to avoid the draft. It seemed that every institution on which the nation had relied to pass on its values was now questioned. Radical student groups like Students for a Democratic Society grabbed headlines, and even more radical groups like the Black Panthers resorted to violence to make their point.

It isn't hard to imagine how unpopular the tepid chapel services of these small, private secondary schools soon became to students forced to sit in straight-backed pews wearing blazers and starched shirts and sing some grand old hymn of the church—or even recite the Apostles' Creed. It didn't help when the headmaster or chaplain intoned about the virtues of responsibility and fair play, the need to find some purpose in life for oneself, or the gratitude we should feel at the privilege of studying at such an august institution as theirs. "We can't take this, and we won't," many said either out loud or under their breath. The innocuous watered-down theology that had undergirded these schools for decades evaporated into thin air. Most schools began to retreat from any form of required religion program, abandoning compulsory chapel and turned study of the Bible into a useful prop for analyzing current events.

Seymour St. John, headmaster of Choate School in Connecticut (where C.R.I.S. had moved its offices at his invitation), was one of the headmasters who felt this opposition particularly keenly. As an ordained clergyman of the "old school," he believed in the value of church as an instrument for good in society. But, whatever he personally believed, he seemed to have abandoned the concept that there was Good News that students needed to hear and respond to. His assistant headmaster Peter Prescott, later the headmaster of Ridley College, wrote *A World Of Our Own*, a particularly uncomfortable expose of the soft underbelly of prep school life. The book posed serious questions about how equipped these noted institutions were to pass on the time-tested values of the past, given the shakeup of that turbulent decade.

1. *The Childress family at Nana and Bomp's 50th Wedding Anniversary*

2. *Mary-Adair (Maizie) Childress Moore*

3. Very young and wet behind the ears

4. Sandra Beatrice Clark Moore

5. Oscar F. Moore with his grandson, David

6. Little Trinity Church, Toronto

7. One of many sports, age 68

8. Hiking in the Grand Tetons, Wyoming: Kate & Sean, David, Sandra and me

9. 606 East Drive, Sewickley

10. Leading a tour in the South of France, 2013

11. With the Peter Clark family at the FOCUS 50th. Reunion, 2011

12. David and Lexi are married, August, 2012

CHAPTER 10

PARA-CHURCH MINISTRY

Interestingly, when I was hired by the Council for Religion the board and staff knew that I had already founded FOCUS. At the time, we were calling it University and Private School Camps, mirroring the somewhat arcane name of the British program that was our model: Varsity and Public School Camps. To the C.R.I.S. board, UPSC or later FOCUS, was an occasional activity that I did in my spare time. None on the board at the time saw it as a threat to the dominance of C.R.I.S., where membership, annual dues, and trustee involvement connected it institutionally to the 300 schools it served. With the knowledge of the C.R.I.S. board, I would hire people to take care of the growing needs of FOCUS, which became our acronym for Fellowship Of Christians in Universities and Schools. Debbie Smyth was the first Secretary of FOCUS. She was followed by Mardi Drew (later Keyes), and soon others were brought on board. They occupied a small innocuous desk in a corner of the C.R.I.S. office. Who at the time would have guessed that tiny FOCUS would eventually become many times the Council's size in budget and staff?

But there were reasons for that. Theological pluralism, with no authority from which to say anything definite, had begun to eat away at the foundations of traditional religion. Membership in the denominations that had hitched their wagons to it was already on the decline. What had sounded radical and chic in the Fifties and Sixties, especially with dynamic spokesmen like Yale chaplain Bill Coffin fueling its fires, had begun to shrivel up and die within a few decades. A major realignment was taking place. The Protestant "mainline" was becoming the new "sideline" while evangelical Christianity was flexing its muscles and exhibiting extraordinary growth. Internationally, the churches of the affluent West were unintentionally passing the baton to the fast-growing churches of the Global South. The dying churches of Europe and North America ceded leadership to the dynamic churches of Africa, Asia, and Latin America. C.R.I.S., and other similar student ministries such as the college-based Student Christian Movement, hung on for a couple of decades, redefining their mission from "religion" to "ethics" to "values." Meanwhile evangelical para-church ministries like Inter-Varsity Christian Fellowship, Campus Crusade for Christ (CRU), The Navigators, and more recently Reformed University Fellowship responded to the hunger of generations of younger students eager for something that spoke to their spiritual quest: Bible study, mentoring, and a social ethic grounded in biblical theology.

FOCUS BUILDS UP STEAM

The early years of FOCUS proved to be largely experimental. Our first event was in June of 1961. In a borrowed Adirondack camp where moose heads greeted one from the walls and bear rugs warmed the floor, we held our first house party. Fifteen people in all—mostly boys from Groton, St. Mark's, Andover, St. Paul's, and Governor Dummer—swam, boated, played tennis, hiked, and heard talks on the Christian faith and life. This kicked off an annual series of ten-day long house parties held at the far-away vacation homes of women who had been touched by the Billy Graham crusades of the late 1950s.

I had met many of these women through Daphne Lacey, who ministered to them on behalf of the Billy Graham organization. An impressive woman with an ebullient personality and a ready laugh, Daphne introduced me to Audrey Clark, and Peggy Taliaferro—both of whom had met Christ through these crusades. Peggy and her husband Champe accepted Christ in Madison Square Garden, barely knowing what they were doing. But God transformed their lives, and Peggy, who died in 2010 well into her nineties, discovered that she had a special vision to lead young people and society women to God through imaginative Bible teaching. She founded groups in Long Island and on Jupiter Island, Florida. It was she, Audrey Clark, and many others, including Eleanor Whitney, Caroline Lynch, Joan Hay, Betty Iglehart, Whitney Atwood, and Maggie Purnell who became a de facto support group for FOCUS. They opened their homes, and to an extent their check books, to help make the ministry happen.

It is hard to underestimate the extraordinary spiritual stir that had taken place among these Long Island women. Most were very wealthy, much-married, and socially-connected. They were the least typical women you might expect to respond to the old-fashioned Gospel preached by the likes of Billy Graham. However, in 1957 Eleanor Whitney (Mrs. Cornelius Vanderbilt Whitney) had invited Billy Graham to her Old Westbury manor, and filled the place with people probably as eager to see her elegant estate as to hear the famous evangelist. But God was on the march. Soon people like Joan Hay were giving their testimony at a ladies' luncheon at the Piping Rock Club. Standing with her heels together in the perfect posture that her blue-blood upbringing had taught her, she shared how God had made himself real to her.

She recalled hearing her first Bible teacher, Beth Paddon, wife of the CEO of Sunshine Biscuits, say to her that "if you were the only person in the world, Jesus Christ would still have died for you." She then said to those stunned women: "I couldn't think of a thing to say, and I still can't." Later Joan Hay (later Madeira) got an M.Div. degree from General Theological Seminary, and opened up a Hospice ministry in Long Island and in Florida.

REACHING THE KIDS

Naturally, these women were concerned to see their sons and daughters discover the new life that they had found. With seemingly boundless resources at their fingertips, their vision nicely merged with my own and soon led to youth parties on Long Island's North Shore with butlers scurrying about with trays of hamburgers while I played games with the teen-aged kids in the pool. After food and games, I would give a talk on why the Christian faith was true and viable. Some would stare in disbelief, while others showed real interest and began coming away with me and my growing team of helpers to one of our summer camps. Many of these young people became believers, but only a few in those early years became strong disciples. One, however, most certainly did.

SANDY

Sandy Clark, daughter of Fritz and Audrey Clark, had made a decision for Christ when her mother, on a whim, brought her to Billy Graham's New York Crusade in 1957. But though it planted a seed, there was little growth to show for it. A few years later, there she was—one of the shiny-faced prep school girls at those Long Island pool parties. Sandy remembers hearing me talk about why Christianity was true, and being quite puzzled. She would soon graduate from St. Timothy's School and head off to Harvard's Radcliffe College, around the time I was coming into my own as Director of the Council for Religion. There at Harvard, she recommitted her life to Christ, with the help of Campus Crusade and became friends with fellow students like Bill Edgar who was later to become—with his wife Barbara—both a dear friend and a noted theologian and author. Soon Sandy was volunteering to lead at FOCUS house parties.

It was hard not to notice her among the crowd. She was very pretty, sensitive, had a coy way about her, and loved to tease. I recall later racing our cars once on a highway headed to New Hampshire for a FOCUS ski week, probably risking life and limb. From these fun experiences I began to wonder if Sandy and I might have a special relationship. On graduation I tried to hire her in C.R.I.S., but her father wisely thought that she needed a broader exposure to the real world. So, instead of working for me, she worked for Harper & Row publishers for a year and then headed off to Europe for further study at Francis Schaeffer's L'Abri community in the Swiss Alps.

While she was there, I discovered the old truism that "Absence makes the heart grow fonder." It was worse. I realized that I had a rival for Sandy's affection. So I took action. We corresponded, and as soon as she returned to the States, I staked my claim: "Do you think that we might begin to see one another and find out of God has something deeper for us?" Of course I remember our first kiss—which was surprisingly unemotional, although the repercussions were deeply felt. We were soon meeting discreetly (since, after all, I was running a growing youth program) and structuring our weeks to be together as much as we could. After a mere six weeks of this, we were clear that God had intended us for one another. Squeezed together on Peggy Taliaferro's couch on Jupiter Island, Florida, while on a short October visit with her parents, Sandy and I got engaged.

Prior to our marriage, Sandy began traveling with me to various prep schools and attending C.R.I.S. conferences. Seeing little fruit coming from all the activity, she strongly urged me to leave C.R.I.S. and launch out full-time with FOCUS. I was not quite ready for that at the time. But eventually I took her advice.

Our marriage took place on December 7th, Pearl Harbor Day, 1968. There was frost on the ground and the Clarks had rented a yellow and white tent to cover their terrace on Valentine Lane, while space heaters took the chill from the air. Friends from FOCUS and C.R.I.S. were present, as were many from our two families. Peter Haile, my first mentor, now chaplain at Stony Brook School, and John Howe, chaplain at Loomis School, married us in St. John's of Lattingtown in Locust Valley. Then, leaving all our friends and family behind at the reception, we were whisked to J.F.K. airport, where we departed for a four-month sabbatical honeymoon in Europe. I had been promised a sabbatical and it made sense to combine that with a honeymoon. So off we flew to Bermuda, London, and the Continent.

SABBATICAL

We soon found ourselves alone, traveling all over Europe in a newly-acquired Volkswagen, attempting to start life together as a married couple. There were humorous moments and I for one felt like a neophyte at the game of marriage. But I found Sandy very supportive and understanding while I made the transition at 32 from chaste bachelorhood to husband. She was also enormously encouraging about the ministry to which we were being called. I soon realized that I had married a woman with a strong mind of her own, a deep spirituality, and great winsomeness with others. Plus, as I said, she was beautiful and fun.

On our honeymoon, I discovered something else about Sandy. She reacted strongly to my obsession with food. I was frankly a voyeur when it came to food, stopping at pastry shop windows in Europe to gawk at the beautiful delicacies so artfully arranged. I noticed that she would freeze and quickly move on. I didn't understand what was happening; but I sensed that she was struggling in some way—not just with my untamed habits, but with a deep problem of her own. Only many years later did I come to accept the dimensions of her struggle with a nagging eating disorder, and still later realize how painful this weakness was to her and how desperate she was to find a way out. I clearly wasn't much help in those early years, driven by my vision for reaching the prep school world. Sandy lived with the tension of my activism, that is my type-A personality, by trying to submit to her husband as she had been taught to do, while quietly struggling to tame the raving beast within.

On the outside, Sandy was the perfect match for me. She proved to be an attractive young Christian wife, capable of serving as a role model for the many young girls who had been drawn to FOCUS. But she found giving talks or leading Bible studies very stressful. She internalized any tension that she sensed around her, and always paid a high price for fatigue. Nevertheless, from the very beginning, she stood by her man and fulfilled my dreams in ways I could never have imagined.

After a quick stop in wind-swept Bermuda, our honeymoon took us to London to see some of Sandy's (by then known everywhere as Sandra) and my old friends from England. We then moved on to Germany, arriving slightly after midnight in Bremen where I had failed to book a hotel. Unfortunately Bremen was hosting a baker's convention and there were virtually no rooms to be had in the city. Sensing our plight, a female flight attendant offered us the room reserved for airline service personnel at the Intercontinental Hotel. The next morning as breakfast was wheeled in on a tray with a rose in a delicate bud vase, we thought we had struck gold—until, unexpectedly, we got the bill.

SWITZERLAND

With the Volkswagen we picked up in Germany, we made our way to Switzerland. There we had a riotous experience on New Year's Eve. We had spent a happy day visiting old friends at L'Abri, Francis Schaeffer's community in the Swiss mountains. But, exhausted, we retired early to the only room available at the local inn—a small bedroom at the top of a winding staircase. After midnight, Sandra woke me up. "There's someone trying to get into our room," she whispered. Sure enough, the door to our room was jiggling, and someone was definitely trying to get in.

We then heard what we thought was a water main break. I rushed out of bed and threw open the door. A drunken Frenchman, in near delirium, had mistaken our door for the door to the bathroom.

Unable to hold all the beer that he had consumed, he had let go with the consequence that Lake Geneva was seeping into our bedroom. "Arrêt, arrêt," I spat out in fractured French. But it was too late.

Finally, we reached our destination, Lausanne, Switzerland. Joe and Grace Brown were living there while Joe worked for the International Fellowship of Evangelical Students. Meanwhile my good friend, Peter Goodwyn-Hudson, who later became the chaplain of Repton School, told me about the Commonwealth and Continental Church Society with which he had connections. Com. & Con., as it was then known, owned and oversaw a number of chapels on the continent of Europe where English-speaking tourists frequently traveled. Since they needed to staff these chapels with Anglican priests during the winter holiday season, they proclaimed me an answer to their prayers. Whether I was or not, their invitation created the perfect ministry for my sabbatical. Sandra and I whisked off to Verbier, where two ski parties of English young adults were holed up in January. I then did a chaplaincy in Zermatt, and finally one in Grindelwald. In exchange for free places to stay and free daily ski passes, I had the responsibility for Sunday services and visiting local clinics to care for English-speaking patients who had fallen sick or been injured on the slopes.

These chaplaincy experiences were so full of fun that we returned a year later to repeat the duty. As the saying goes: "Someone has to do it." It was on the second of these visits that a remarkable encounter took place. St. Peter's Anglican Church is snuggled into the picturesque alpine village of Zermatt. Carved into the beams that surround its sanctuary you will find the names of famous mountain climbers who lost their lives trying to scale the Matterhorn in the earliest days of mountaineering. On that January Sunday in 1970, as I preached, one face stood out in the crowd. The young man was tall, had long blond hair, and he was listening intensely to my sermon. I had filled the sermon with quotes from gloomy Existential writers but included at the end just enough Good News to spark his interest. It turned out to be Bob Kramer, who had dropped out of Harvard, was wandering around Europe, and was only in church that day to hear some English spoken. In a hitherto vain effort to find himself, upon reading many of the same writers I had just quoted, he had concluded that all life was absurd. After a two-hour conversation, he said something I've never forgotten: "I always knew Christians had faith, but I never knew that they had answers."

At my suggestion, Bob went to L'Abri. There Dr. Francis Schaeffer, his wife, and others, including Os Guinness, held sway amid a steady stream of wandering students from around the world, seeking answers to life's questions. Both Sandra and I had spent time there prior to our marriage and, as I mentioned, we had paid a brief visit on our honeymoon. After two months of resisting the simple message of God's love, Bob decided, in a conversation with Edith Schaeffer, to give faith a try. His life was turned around. He returned to finish Harvard where he had formerly been president of Students for a Democratic Society, the radical student group that had led demonstrations in front of the President of Harvard's house and where he had also begun extensive experimentation with drugs. He graduated, went to seminary, and eventually was led into politics and business. During this time, Bob became a volunteer in FOCUS, along with many others who had been touched at L'Abri. Then—if you fast-forward the clock several decades—his and his wife Diane's daughter, Daria, became one of FOCUS' most effective field staff. God works in wonderful and mysterious ways.

CHAPTER 11

CONNECTICUT

FOCUS TAKES OFF

When I finally listened seriously to Sandra, I realized it was time to leave C.R.I.S. and move to FOCUS. I was reluctant because my meager salary with C.R.I.S. seemed less trouble than raising a director's salary for FOCUS, in addition to a secretary's. It was more than my untrusting mind could fathom. But Sandra had faith, and her faith bolstered my own. Of course, I was deeply aware of the fact that, as an impecunious young clergyman working for an even more impecunious organization, I could never earn enough to support her as well as start a family. But with help from Sandra's parents we were able to live where we needed to and to devote ourselves to the ministry without fretting about where the next meal was coming from.

We moved first of all from New York City to a small rented house in Wallingford, Connecticut. On the way, we carefully stashed all our worldly goods in a U-Haul truck and headed for our new home. Just as we were passing New Haven on the Interstate, I began to hear other motorists honking at me. Finally they caught my attention, and when I looked out the rear view mirror I saw the left two wheels of the truck slowly extending from the vehicle. In a minute or less, they would have fallen off and the truck would have capsized. Just in the nick of time, with a brake malfunction, I coasted to a stop and phoned U-Haul, in desperation, for help. They arrived and made what seemed a very minor adjustment, and we continued on our way. But I never rented a U-Haul again!

After a year in our rented house, we purchased an 1840s made over farmhouse in nearby Cheshire. It was while we were living in Cheshire that I finally made my break with C.R.I.S. and with a sense of relief coupled with some anxiety committed myself to FOCUS full-time.

PAWLING CAMPS

Meanwhile, the annual round of FOCUS "camps" were beginning to bear extraordinary fruit. We did our best to call these events house parties, but the phrase never stuck. We moved from using people's vacation homes to a new location in Pawling—a town made famous by Norman Vincent Peale, the best-selling author of *The Power of Positive Thinking.* He owned and operated a huge spread on nearby Quaker Hill. Our first location there was Carroll Lodge—a place that seemed nearly perfect, although the proprietor managed to disrupt our meetings by going to the bar and mixing himself a martini at the most inappropriate moments. We then found Holiday Hills, a YMCA camp in the village of Pawling that consisted of a series of red barns converted into dormitories and meeting rooms. The price and location were fine; however, the facilities were not suited to the learning environment we were trying to create. It required a full two days of brave efforts by Sandra and other volunteers to turn what one leader called "a shabby rural slum" into something warm and welcoming.

Our Pawling FOCUS camps were remarkable in many ways. Students could come and go, especially if they had a major after-school party to attend, They might arrive late from New York City, or leave early. The whole setting was rustic and informal, though never far from civilization. On warm nights, we permitted students to sleep out in sleeping bags on the nearby hill, as long as a couple of seasoned leaders were with them. Parents occasionally complained about a general permissiveness, but in the 1960s and early 1970s, we felt the way to reach the young was not through repressive rules but through Spirit-inspired freedom.

Our home in Cheshire had a living room large enough for two fire places, so it proved to be a great local rallying place for the emerging FOCUS ministry. At the time, the Choate Chaplain, Mark Mullin, was running a thriving Christian fellowship. At Loomis-Chaffee School, just north of Hartford, John and Karen Howe were preaching the Gospel to eager students, much to the embarrassment of the school's more humanistic headmaster. One long-term faculty member there, lifelong bachelor Dave Simpson, was converted from skepticism and soon became a FOCUS mainstay. He shepherded the group at Loomis for years to come. Meanwhile, on the other side of Hartford at Ethel Walker's, there was Whitey Haugan, a somewhat zany Episcopal priest serving as chaplain. Whitey's unusual style and theology later became thoroughly grounded in New Testament Christianity, and over the decades to come his later impact as rector of a dynamic parish in Jacksonville, Florida was legendary. Our Cheshire house served as the location of committee meetings, and also as a place for overnight retreats for dozens of students. A few well-known speakers like John Stott made appearances at our Cheshire home to give after-dinner talks to eager students from the entire area. John

Howe eventually became bishop of Central Florida, and Mark Mullin the head of St. Alban's School in D.C.

FAMILY BLESSINGS

During these Cheshire years (1969-1974) Jen was born. She brought sunshine into our lives from the moment she appeared in the Yale-New Haven Hospital. Sandra lay in the room, with Jennifer Clark Moore in her arms. On a table next to her was a meager geranium plant that I—ever tight with money—had purchased in my haste to get back to the hospital after the late-night birth. It was just my luck that across the room from her lay another new mom. Her corner was festooned with roses and other expensive flowers.

Like most new parents, we were not prepared for the challenges of raising a little one. On one occasion, Jen managed to rock her baby carriage so vigorously that it fell onto the stone base of our fireplace. She struck her head as it hit bottom. Frantically, Sandra called the doctor who, upon hearing the full story, recommended a stiff drink—for the mother! Our next-door neighbors (through a path in the garden) were a friendly older couple whom Jen felt free to visit whenever she wished. One warm day she arrived at their home completely naked.

Independent-minded as always, Jen resisted being confined to her crib. Many nights she would manage to climb out of it and crawl down the hall towards the stairs. Usually we caught her before she careened down the uncarpeted staircase. There was the day, however, when we found her surreptitiously creeping along the hallway on her belly so as not to be seen. Fortunately, Sandra's shrewd eye caught her just in time.

The addition to our family of Jennifer, to whom I soon gave the diminutive nickname Jennabug, gave Sandra a new focus of attention. She threw herself into motherhood with zeal, developing relationships with one or two neighborhood mothers who had little tots of their own. From the start Jen had a very loving and giving disposition. We, of course, doted on her, and tried our best to be responsible parents.

Our house in Cheshire was extraordinary. The large living room was a combination of three rooms and had wood beams in the ceiling and wide floorboards. We added a handsome bay window overlooking the garden. Its surrounding acre of lawn was endowed with several perennial gardens, large lilac bushes, and some huge vintage maples—one of which came crashing down in a hurricane, bruising the rooftop and damaging my study while we watched. Thanks to Sandra's brother Peter Clark's skillful use of a chain saw, and Fritz Clark's encouragement, we scooped up most of the lumber for future fires, and soon the house was back in shape.

Being a young couple with only one child, and living more or less in the center of New England in a large house, we soon became a *Mecca* for Christian groups and events. We began a series of theological conferences for college students, held at Yale, and grabbed noted speakers like Os Guinness, N.T. Wright, and John Stott when they were in the area. Sometimes these conferences would include as many as 50 young adults and they often ended with a large dinner at our house. I recall Sandra putting together huge meals with wine and, at my request, an elegant trifle for dessert.

The large lawn and established gardens of this country house took a great deal of care, as did the exterior of the house. But it was a place I will always remember fondly. I cried quietly when we finally sold it and moved to Stamford. Would we ever live in such a delightful place again?

One of the reasons for our move was that Cheshire afforded very few potential friends for Sandra in the immediate neighborhood, and we could find no church where there was real fellowship. At the suggestion of Bill and Barbara Edgar we decided to sell our beloved 496 Cook Hill Road and move to Fairfield County. There we would be closer to the real center of our ministry that had expanded from New England down to Philadelphia and soon Baltimore, and we would be closer to Christian fellowship and a good church.

THE CALL TO COMMUNITY

It was in the second year of our marriage that Sandra and I observed how easy it was for students who had been deeply touched by God at our various house parties to fall away once they returned to their families, school friends, or summer vacation places. As we talked about this together, it was clear that there was a need for a place where these students could experience Christian community, far from the distractions and temptations of their former lives.

The FOCUS Committee at that point consisted of Sam and Edith Abbott, Dave Simpson, Dick and Mardi Keyes, Debbie Smyth, Chris and Franny Keidel, George Gentsch, and others. At a meeting we agreed that we should find a way to replicate the L'Abri emphasis on community in order to hold on to these young Christian students and help them towards maturity. Interestingly, each of these early FOCUS visionaries later had distinguished and noted ministries as teachers, authors, rectors, missionaries and heads of organizations. And already, their future leadership gifts brought depth and wisdom to the solid foundation under the emerging FOCUS work.

During 1970 and 1971, Sandra and I spent two summers in a large rented house on Martha's Vineyard that was opened to all comers. I taught tennis at the Chilmark Community Center, where Whitey Haugan was the summer Director. We rented out our apartment in Manhattan. The income from those two ventures, plus a few gifts from family and friends, covered the cost of the house at Gay Head and the expenses of providing meals for visitors. A steady stream of students arrived at our lonely outpost on the westernmost promontory of the Vineyard. We counseled them, taught the Bible to them, welcomed them to our table, and in a variety of ways gave ourselves to them. One of the most remarkable stories to come from those summers was the conversion of George Wadsworth. He had graduated from Middlesex, having been raised in a skeptical family, and found his way almost by accident to our compound. George quickly came to full Christian commitment, was baptized in the waves below our rented house, and later, with his wife, became a missionary to one of the poorest parts of the Caribbean.

And who could forget Siggy Gross, a Columbia University student who dropped in on our Gay Head ménage planning on a short visit but ended up staying for several weeks? Siggy had caught wind that there was a cheap place to stay overnight way out in Gay Head, and hitchhiked the 24 miles from the ferry to us. His Jewish background and questioning mindset had not prepared him for anything resembling the kind of Bible study or Christian discussion that took place around our table at meal times. But with his curiosity peaked, Siggy began to read the New Testament. This only led to a further barrage of questions about Old Testament prophecy and the like. By the end of the summer he was genuinely interested and decided to attend our Labor Day weekend "camp" back in Pawling. I still remember him listening attentively to all the talks that outlined the basic ideas of the Christian faith and the call to commit oneself to Christ.

In those days we usually ended our week-long house parties with a very informal service of Holy Communion. As I explained the service, I made it clear that this was a feast for believers. But I also said that any who wanted to commit their lives to Christ in the process of taking Communion could come and do so. There was both a solemnity and a joy about these occasions, because they brought us all back to the early church's experience of the Last Supper and to the Cross. This time, I noticed when the Communion was over that Siggy had not come forward to take the bread or the wine. But then, after everyone had left the room, he emerged out of the shadows and looked straight at me across the Holy Table, and with a firm voice said: "Peter, Jesus told me to take some bread." I offered him the bread and wine, and he received it. The change in him was noticeable from that moment on, and some months later it was my privilege to baptize him among FOCUS friends in the Ethel Walker School chapel. He later went on to study at the Hebrew University in Jerusalem.

THE PHONE CALL THAT CHANGED EVERYTHING

With the experience of our two summers at Gay Head behind us, thanks to the help of our small team that included Neil and Marsha Lebhar [Neil was later to become a bishop in the Anglican Church of North America], and others, we were primed to see the importance of community to the future of the FOCUS vision. But where to go, and what to do? It was after a lengthy Committee meeting in Cheshire, at which we all reiterated our conviction that community was essential, that I received a call from Whitney Atwood. It left me stunned. Whitney lived next door to Sandra's parents on Long Island.

As a younger woman, she had gone to Hollywood to be in pictures for a short time. Her checkered life involved three husbands, by one of whom she had a son, Tim Choate. But Whitney was one of those Long Island ladies who had caught the vision of FOCUS. In fact, it was she who had invited Audy Clark to her very first Bible study at her house. Audy, who at that time thought the only place for religion to be talked about was in church, wearing a proper dress. She warily asked Whitney, "May I wear slacks?"

Whitney Atwood persisted in her unique and unconventional witness to friends on Long Island. It was our good fortune that from the earliest days she was energetically supportive of everything we were doing. The day I received a call from her, she asked me: "Peter, how would you like the gift of 21 acres and a barn and hunting lodge on Martha's Vineyard?" I was speechless. Now, more than 40 years later, we can see how God was in that offer. Indeed the whole vision to go to Martha's Vineyard originally came to us when on a ferry from Nantucket Sandra had read Psalm 80, verses 8 and 9: "Thou didst bring a vine out of Egypt…It took deep root and filled the land." The sense of God's leading was as clear as anything I can remember in my life.

It is hard, in retrospect, to imagine the magnitude of Whitney Atwood's offer. Here was property, perfectly situated on the very Island to which we had originally been called by Sandra's interpretation of Psalm 80, literally handed to us gratis. Of course we had doubts. How, with a tiny budget, and me still at that point working for C.R.I.S., could FOCUS possibly afford to maintain such a place, much less turn it into a location where large numbers of students might come and stay?

That March a group of us went to explore the property. We found it so badly overgrown from years of neglect that the poison ivy covering its buildings had bark on it. Moreover there were only two very impractical buildings, and both needed a great deal of work. Nevertheless, the location was perfect, and the possibilities limitless. We gratefully received the gift and that summer, and for a couple of summers afterwards, groups of hearty volunteers including Hillary Bercovici, Eric Winter, George Gentsch, Becky Drew, Dave Simpson, Dick Ferguson, Woody Bowman and many others descended upon what we eventually named the FOCUS Study Center. Our first summer presented us with a major challenge: clear the site and turn the two buildings into something useable. By August we felt ready enough to receive our first contingent of eager students—most of whom camped out in tents. Little did we know then that this place would become a spiritual home for thousands of independent school students and their friends in the decades to come. But with high hopes for the future, we dedicated the property to God in a simple but dignified ceremony. Today, as I write, it is an almost luxurious facility on now 44 acres with nine fine buildings, plenty of soft green grass, a lakefront on Uncle Seth's Pond, tennis courts, and comely gardens. Who would have thought it in those nascent days of 1973?

CHAPTER 12

RENEWAL IN THE CHURCH

DARIEN

Part of the lure of Fairfield County to which we had moved was the buzz of activity surrounding St. Paul's Church. Under the leadership of the Rev. "Terry" Fullam, St. Paul's, a small suburban parish situated in Darien, one of New York City's leafier suburbs, had experienced exponential growth and spiritual renewal. People were making their way from all over the Northeast to hear him preach and to see an Episcopal church in revival. After selling Cheshire, we moved into a modified colonial ranch house in the northern suburbs of Stamford, Connecticut. The location put us near the Merritt Parkway and a mere hop, skip, and jump from St. Paul's. In addition, it allowed us to send Jen to nearby Greenwich Academy, although we first tried local public schools. The latter proved too stress-producing, because of the presence of some bullying. Fortunately, the house we purchased had a large finished basement that provided excellent office space for the FOCUS ministry. Soon 137 Red Fox Road became the new address both for the Moores and FOCUS.

St. Paul's in Darien began opening my eyes to the second part of the vision God gave me as a young man: to leave a vibrant biblical remnant in the Episcopal Church. Given the entrepreneurial mindset I inherited from my mother, I was always spotting a need that was not being filled. When it came to the Episcopal Church, it was easy to see such need. Having reading E. Clowes Chorley's book *Men and Movements in the American Episcopal Church,* I could see how the denomination in which I was ordained had in the mid and late 19th century turned its back on the Evangelicalism that characterized many of its most vigorous early years. Several of its theological seminaries like Virginia, Bexley Hall, and even the Episcopal Theological School that I had attended had at one time characterized themselves as "Evangelical" in the broadest sense of the word. But each of them, by the 20th century had in one degree or another succumbed to the spell of liberal Protestantism.

I knew from my own seminary experience how daunting it was to run the gauntlet of liberal theology. I knew that if it had been tough for me, it would be even tougher for those less grounded in Scripture than I. But what would we do now with the spiritual renewal gaining momentum and with many men and soon women seeking solid places to be trained for the ordained ministry? In the absence of any place I could find in the Episcopal Church, I began directing friends towards Oxford University. Several followed, including John Evans, Bob Sellers, Tom Oates, and Mark Berner. This situation only made me see the great need that existed for a place within the Episcopal Church where evangelical fellowship could be nurtured, and where students could be trained for a biblically-based, mission-minded ministry.

The groundwork had already been laid for this intention with the formation of an American branch of the Evangelical Fellowship in the Anglican Communion. With the help of Philip Edgecombe Hughes and Stuart Barton Babbage, both noted Anglican theologians who had been invited to teach at Columbia Seminary in Georgia, and with my own growing contacts we formed E.F.A.C.—USA. Later, for a period, it was renamed The Fellowship Of Witness. This small but growing fellowship gathered renewal-minded Episcopalians to a series of conferences that were full of life and promise. Thanks to the periodic visits of high-profile leaders like John Stott and Jim Packer, biblical believers were coming out of the woodwork all over the Episcopal Church. The Fellowship Of Witness started a magazine and with the growing activity soon there was a steady stream of candidates eager to study for the ministry.

CHARISMATIC CHRISTIANITY

This evangelical resurgence coincided with a similar, but slightly different, charismatic movement. Fueled by Pentecostal preachers from abroad, and inspired by the American-based Pentecostal movement emerging from California in the early 20th century. To everyone's surprise Episcopalians began to discover speaking in tongues, healing, and other gifts and manifestations of the Spirit. Whole congregations were caught up in this lively movement, most notably St. Paul's. Even *TIME* Magazine got a whiff of what was happening in this affluent suburb filled with executives and professionals. A book entitled *Miracle in Darien* documenting the remarkable work of God only fanned the flames.

Terry Fullam's preaching style enthralled Bible-ignorant Episcopalians. With great skill, he would string a group of Bible verses together on a theme, and make the theme come alive. While I appreciated his evident gifts, I had been exposed to a different way of expounding Scripture. In England, preachers usually stuck with one text and opened it in such a way that its riches were discovered and its underlying message applied. I missed that approach in Terry Fullam's preaching, even though I recognized the obvious blessing of God on his ministry. Eventually, however, I was so starved for what I understood as good expository preaching that I began to wonder if I could do it myself. That yearning eventually catapulted me out of student ministry entirely, and into a parish.

But before I leave these remarkable times, I need to share my own encounter with the charismatic movement. Partly because of my leadership in FOCUS, I had to decide for myself whether I could wholeheartedly affirm this new movement or not. Some of our leaders had discovered the more dramatic gifts of the Holy Spirit themselves, and were eager to move FOCUS in a charismatic direction. John and (especially) Karen Howe were key figures in this effort, and they linked hands with Renny Scott, a dynamic young Episcopal priest whom I had hired to work in the boarding schools of New England. Renny and I had become friends during his final year at E.T.S. in Cambridge, and he had fallen in love with the FOCUS ministry. No one was able to hold an entire room full of students so enthralled with a Gospel talk as he. During his two years on our small staff he cut quite a figure: articulate, spiritually incendiary, and very personable. Unfortunately, he also had an unpredictable side to his character that I was concerned might veer toward extremism.

Later he became Rector of the prestigious St. Phillips Church in Charleston, South Carolina where, in the middle of a sermon, he revealed that for years a woman he had mistreated had put a "hex" on him and that it had dogged his steps ever since. He walked out of the pulpit and disappeared out the back door. He quickly vanished from Charleston almost without a trace. Major news magazines picked up the story. Later, the ever-resourceful Renny surfaced in Atlanta, and began a new ministry.

Because of the outbreak of charismatic Christianity within FOCUS, our leadership core spent considerable time thinking through our corporate response. I read books on all sides of the issue, as did others. In the end we concluded that, while these manifestations were most likely genuine gifts of the Spirit, the theology that often promoted them, a biblical exegesis stressing "baptism in the Holy Spirit" as a second work of grace, could not be supported. We wrote a "white paper" and moved forward, welcoming all who would agree with what we trusted was a balanced position.

SKI WEEKS

By now, FOCUS was sponsoring a fairly well-organized round of annual activities. These had expanded from summer events to a series of winter ski weeks held over the New Year. The first of these ski weeks was unforgettable. Helen Gibson, mother of the redoubtable Whitney Atwood, had invited us to use her North Conway, New Hampshire, house as our base. Helen's husband, Harvey D. Gibson, a wealthy New Yorker who in 1921 had helped form the New York Trust Company, owned a great deal of land in the vicinity of Cranmore Mountain. In the late 1930s he had secured the release of Johann "Hannes" Schneider from an Austrian prison (paying Hitler a handsome ransom, so the story went) and deposited the skiing ace in North Conway. There Schneider began teaching Americans the Austrian way of skiing: fixed bindings, parallel skis, and Christie turns. This soon became the new American way. Schneider later taught the Japanese these same methods.

Helen, whose glamorous estate overlooked Long Island Sound, decided to preside, herself, over our first ski week right there at her North Conway home. She ordered the butler to serve up roast beef and Yorkshire pudding on New Year's Eve and to treat us all to free ski lessons from Schneider's son, Herbert. Herbert Schneider, who I suspect was used to elegant well-dressed guests emerging from Helen Gibson's home, tried his best to figure out what this unlikely group of young adults was doing in her house. We did not have proper ski attire, and we were nearly all beginners. To him, we must have looked like quite a ragamuffin crew. Finally the eminent ski pro managed to come up with a category into which to put our slightly unkempt group: "Charity."

Winter Ski Weeks, as these were soon called, became a staple of the FOCUS ministry and continue to his day. Through these events, innumerable boys and girls have had their first encounter with the Christian message, presented in a lively and attractive way. Over the years, these ski adventures located themselves in a variety of conference centers including the never-to-be-forgotten Gray Ledges in Grantham, New Hampshire to the commodious and large YMCA hotel in Lake George, New York. At one point we had three separate FOCUS Winter House Parties running concurrently over the New Year, including a Colorado Rocky Mountain option for the stout -hearted.

The owner of Gray Ledges, where we went for years, Carol Sturgis, was one of the most unforgettable characters I've ever met. Carol would covertly seek to initiate students to the wonders of charismatic Christianity right under our noses, and seemed totally oblivious to the sensitive nature of our work, given that so many students came from unbelieving homes. Moreover, her facility, a made-over farm, was prone to sudden power outages and water shortages causing the camps frequently to do without—a rather difficult thing to do in sub-zero weather with over 100 young people needing to eat and use the toilet! Nevertheless, Gray Ledges will always be remembered by many as the place where some amazing life-changes happened.

In addition to secondary school students, I was concerned to reach college students, particularly at leading New England colleges. So we began a series of Skis and Skeptics Weekends for college students. These ran for several years and bore significant fruit. They tended to attract those who were not what might be called "religious types." But, thanks to the working of God's Spirit, many who were at first drawn by great fun and engaging sports responded to our matter-of-fact approach to the Gospel. The name caught on and soon we were running Skis and Skeptics Weekends in the midwinter for students from New England prep schools as well. I recall one of them when a busload of boys came to Gray Ledges from a boarding school in Connecticut. After the talk on the first evening one student, Fritz Feick, decided to follow Christ. Later I overheard one of his fellow students confide to another: "They got Fritz!" Clearly, the boys had been warned to beware of these eager evangelists from FOCUS!

THE TURBULENT SIXTIES

The 1960's were truly extraordinary times. The high water mark of the turbulence that characterized this decade was the Woodstock Festival in 1969—a gathering of half a million young adults held on a farm in upstate New York that *Rolling Stone* magazine said "changed the history of Rock music." But the decade embodied a general spirit of lawlessness, anti-authoritarianism and hedonism, all fueled by the deeply troubling war in Viet Nam. One of the chief apologists for the radical left-leaning worldview that the decade promoted was Yale's chaplain Bill Coffin. Bright, brash, with an impeccable academic pedigree, Coffin was the darling of most of the prep school chaplains with whom we regularly interacted. He was a much sought after chapel speaker, and was frequently chosen by the chaplains as a speaker at C.R.I.S. conferences.

Coffin had earned his spurs marching with Martin Luther King in Alabama, had a stable of war stories, and could sit at the piano and belt out Russian songs at the drop of a hat. Unfortunately, while his persona was full of braggadocio, his Christian sympathies were decidedly unorthodox. At a C.R.I.S. Conference for school heads in Washington, D.C. in 1965, he ridiculed former U.N. Secretary-General Charles Malik when he shared his earnest Christ-centered faith and critiqued some of Coffin's favorite theologians. Malik, who had drafted the now-famous United Nations Declaration of Human Rights, was able to give back as well as he got. I made sure that the unflattering banter these two luminaries shot back and forth was adequately reported in a Seabury Press book I edited entitled *Youth In Crisis (1966).* Bill Coffin was fond of one-liners like "small Christian schools produce small Christians." His first wife had been the daughter of the famed pianist Arthur Rubinstein, and once, when he was compared to Billy Graham, Coffin said it was like comparing Rubenstein to Liberace—a virtuoso to an oozy popularizer, not to be taken seriously. Doubtless Bill Coffin looked askance at our efforts to present biblical Christianity in a new light, thinking himself to be countercultural. It was we, however, who were the true counterculture. Coffin represented the mainstream thinking of the Ivy League colleges (and the prep schools that fed them). We, on the other hand, were engaged in an underground mission that may have appeared conformist on the outside, but was actually profoundly countercultural inside.

MULTI-MEDIA SHOWS

Among our more innovative efforts, during these early years when I was transitioning from C.R.I.S. to FOCUS, was the production of a series of multi-media shows. It was Twenty-One Hundred, Inter-Varsity's creative multi-media presentation that gave the idea to Nan Gardner, a graduate of Windsor School and the University of Vermont. Nan came on staff and began to create her own series of shows. Using six integrated slide projectors and large speakers that projected dialogue and background music, the shows were powerful statements of Christian truth mediated through testimony, strong visuals, and contemporary music.

Nan would lug all this equipment around from school to school and perform her shows to eager audiences. One show included a personal testimony by newly-converted Charles Colson, the Watergate convict, whom Nan and I interviewed for over an hour in his Washington home. In addition, thanks to the vision of Thomas F. Staley and his Foundation, FOCUS received grant monies with which to bring impressive speakers to schools. School heads and chaplains were delighted to welcome articulate speakers like Ernest Gordon, Dean of the Chapel at Princeton, one of several we recruited. We also staged concerts at various schools to raise awareness of world hunger. Gifted field staff like Tom Oates and Chip Morgan, both products of the ministry, enhanced the growing image of FOCUS as an organization of substance capable of attracting highly educated and gifted staff. In those days, in an effort to bridge the world of the Bible and contemporary culture, I might give a talk at a school that included brief recordings of familiar songs from *Godspell* or *Jesus Christ Superstar*.

With the move from central Connecticut to Fairfield County, the heart of the ministry of FOCUS shifted. Following the success we had seen in the boarding schools of New England, we discovered a ready new audience in the private day schools that dotted the major cities and suburbs up and down the East Coast, as far south as Washington and ultimately Richmond and Raleigh. Our office in Stamford was a good staging point for this new thrust into the day schools. Staff workers like Richard Gwathmey, Tom Oates, Chip Morgan, Charlie Drew, Gary Niels, Ross Kimball, Dudley Cleghorn, and Phil Lyman came on board and brought remarkable speaking and pastoral gifts that added luster and credibility to the ministry as it expanded to an ever-widening circle of students and parents.

Naturally, all this activity and new staffing required more money. My job as Director gradually changed from program manager to chief administrator, and then chief fundraiser. Initially, our board of trustees had consisted of friends of the ministry, not seasoned individuals with experience in the world of non-profits. In some cases their loyalties were to individual staff rather than to FOCUS as a whole. This meant that when staff felt the burden of the work, and especially the difficult task of fundraising the board's sympathies were aroused. When they eyed my circle of affluent Christians who had come to see the importance of reaching tomorrow's leaders, it became easy for these trustees and staff to think "Peter can raise the money while the rest of us get on with the ministry." This situation produced tension. It seemed that I was expected to provide for an ever-growing budget while inwardly I yearned to do more hands-on ministry. My restlessness was compounded by the fact that former FOCUS colleagues were now branching out and exercising ministries that reached ever widening circles of people. Also, since I had been one of the founders of Trinity Episcopal School for Ministry and its first board chair, I felt pulled ever further away from the high school-aged students who had been my own primary concern.

CHAPTER 13

GREENWICH

During our Stamford sojourn, Catharine Mackay Moore was born. We painted her room lavender, and Mary MacFadden, the Clark's faithful maid flew up from Florida to help us in the early days of caring for a newborn. Ever a loving child, and easy to raise, Kate brightened up a room whenever she appeared. She was the kind of person to whom others warmed, especially as she entered school. Sandra busied herself with the children's activities that soon included ballet and horseback riding. Jen was our ballet dancer, while Kate would eventually take a shine to horses.

We moved to Greenwich in order to be closer to the school we had chosen for the girls. Our house on Kenilworth Terrace has since disappeared because the land was more valuable than the building on it. But for us it was delightful. Sandra decorated it with bright colors, and even when an earthquake startled us all at 7:00 one morning, we felt it was sturdy, attractive and cozy.

We continued to welcome groups of students during vacation times and host small Bible study groups in our home. One very bright student from Brunswick School, Todd Hartch, brought his inquiring mind to these meetings. I recall, during a study of the Gospel of John, that the scales figuratively fell from his eyes as he suddenly realized that Jesus was actually the Son of God. His parents, an established

Greenwich family, at first seemed rather concerned. But eventually they became supportive and recently told me how they had both become committed and active believers.

One of the local Greenwich boys who had become involved in FOCUS was Allen Lovejoy. After a wild youth that involved inappropriate behavior with drugs and girls, Allen found a home within the FOCUS orbit, serving on our Martha's Vineyard staff as a maintenance man for several summers. While a true follower of Christ, Allen found that the pull of the world continually dogged his steps. I sought to mentor him and we became close friends, often camping and hiking in adventuresome places like New Hampshire's White Mountains or climbing Maine's famed Knife Edge. Despite some major bumps in the road, he matured and began to play a very active role in his local Presbyterian church. It was a great relief to me when he found Lorain, a wise Christian woman from the area, to marry. As I write, their three grown daughters are all strong in the faith and pursuing marriage and responsible careers.

CHRISTIAN COUNTER-CULTURE

But the larger picture of what was happening was that a renewed expression of the Christian faith was going mainstream. During the first half of the 20th Century, this sort of faith had been the province of smaller evangelical sects, but it was now running full spate through mainline Protestant Churches. Being an overt committed Christian was no longer totally "un-cool". Everywhere it seemed noted celebrities were confessing faith, including such unlikely converts as Bob Dylan and Noel Paul Stookey (of the acclaimed folk group *Peter, Paul and Mary*). Jesus himself made the covers of both LIFE and TIME Magazines. Parents of newly enthused children would scratch their heads: "Drugs I understand; but what's with Jesus?" Part of their concern was entirely valid because a growing number of predatory cults emerged, causing parents to be afraid that their children would be "snapped" up by them. Ever so gradually, the word "Christian" no longer referred to up-tight, buttoned-down conservative Protestants typically saying their prayers in a stained-glass-windowed church somewhere. It now meant following Jesus Christ, and being unashamed about it. It even meant having gone to good schools and colleges, and having embarked on solid professions. One of those professions that saw an influx of the newly-converted was the ordained ministry. Increasing numbers of young men (and women) sensed God's call to full-time ministry in and through the churches. At one point I counted nearly 200 "graduates" of FOCUS who had gone into ministry (at least for a period of time). Many of them went to seminary and were ordained. Thankfully, that number continues to grow.

Near the Study Center on Martha's Vineyard lived a Roman Catholic family that owned the Lambert's Cove Inn, just a short walk through the woods from us. The owners became concerned when their charismatic college-aged Catholic son began coming over to our events in the evenings for encouragement and fellowship. Fearing we were a cult, they stirred up their Vineyard neighbors with lurid rumors of wild events occurring on our property. When we applied for a permit from the Town of West Tisbury to build a couple of simple tent platforms to welcome more students they called for a town meeting. To parry the accusations, several of us who were ordained put on our clerical collars, drew in some respected friends who had summer homes on the Vineyard, and arrived at the meeting with confidence. When the suspicious family saw us, cleaned-up and looking rather established, they slunk into the background. Nothing was heard from them again!

FAMILY TAKES CENTER STAGE

Now that we were firmly ensconced in suburbia, with two daughters in private school, and a recognized organization reaching dozens of schools and hundreds of students annually, it was time for reassessment.

Sandra and I became involved in an exciting home group that grew out of St. Paul's Church. I was invited to teach in the St. Paul's lay Institute and began receiving invitations to speak fairly widely. We even considered joining one of the local country clubs so that I could play tennis. We studied plans that would append an addition to our house. But our stay in Greenwich was not to last long.

I had already begun to look beyond FOCUS. Something was clearly stirring inside me. When I looked at teenagers in the Greenwich area I was not impressed. Listlessness, boredom, recreational drug and alcohol abuse and sexual experimentation were far too common among them, surrounded as they were by seductive affluence. As we thought of our children growing up in this vortex of adolescent corruption, we were not encouraged. In addition, some members of the Board of FOCUS wondered if my own interests were widening too much. As key staff resigned and moved on, I began to question my own commitment to FOCUS long term. Things seemed to be unraveling. I began to think that the time to move on had come.

TENSIONS

There were tensions in the ministry, and it would be too easy to attribute them to the usual stresses when organizations grow from a central administration to ones with regional offices and regional supporters. Whatever the reasons, these tensions made board and staff meetings uncomfortable. I am not sure that the unrest was visible to the students at our camps. But the sheer fun had gone out of working for an emerging ministry. On a gray summer afternoon I took a long walk on a lonely Vineyard beach and realized, sadly, that the time had come to make a move.

Leaving not only the ministry I had founded, but also the area where I had grown up, was hard. Thanksgivings had become family affairs once again, with aunts and uncles coming to our house. Christmas traditions involved being with Sandra's parents who were still living a short distance away on Long Island. Plus my brother-in-law, Peter Clark, was now married to Allison and lived nearby in Westport. It seemed that we were all "coming together" in an ideal way. All of that was soon to be shattered by my decision to leave FOCUS and seek God's leading for a new ministry.

I was aware of the old adage, originally applicable to English schoolmasters, "He who remains a man among boys eventually becomes a boy among men." I felt I needed to grow, and could not see myself remaining in FOCUS until retirement. At 50 I felt that the time had come for a transition.

Without any clear guidance as to precisely where we were being led, I tendered my resignation from FOCUS in 1984, and agreed to complete that school year prior to beginning a sabbatical. Part of the pain of leaving FOCUS was that I wondered (wrongly, as it turned out) if the organization could survive without me. Others shared that feeling, thinking that FOCUS *was* Peter Moore. But nonetheless, I felt that I had made the right decision.

SABBATICAL

With no clear plans for the future, it was inevitable that my sabbatical, beginning late in the spring of 1984, would be difficult. I searched for a parish-based job, but none obviously presented itself. Sandra and I had put five requests before God in prayer: first, that whatever church we might be called to would be open to biblical faith and spiritual renewal. Second, that we would be able to own our own house, and third, be free to send our children to good nearby schools. Fourth, I felt that I needed a full-time assistant. And, finally, we believed we belonged in or near a major metropolitan area. The one request that we forgot to mention was that it be in the United States!

That summer we took a family trip to Europe. Along with Bill and Barb Edgar, we stayed in an apartment north of Barcelona on loan from some English friends whose daughter had stayed with us in Greenwich. We all then journeyed to a small medieval Tuscan town and visited friends of the Edgars who had a large modernized manor house built into the ancient town's wall. Leaving the Edgars there, we took our rented car to Venice, and then boarded the Orient Express bound for London. Jen was just turning 14, and Kate was only 7, and the Orient Express had an amazing deal that enabled both girls to travel absolutely free. We departed Venice for Innsbruck in grand style, spent three days in Austria, and then boarded the Orient Express again for the remainder of the journey. On this trip I even managed to ski on a glacier in midsummer in Austria. Exposing our daughters to some of the wonders of Europe aboard this mysterious train turned the occasion into an unforgettable event. To prepare ourselves we, had watched the 1974 movie, *Murder On The Orient Express*, based on Agatha Christie's famous novel. Our imaginations were so aroused that we fully expected Hercule Poirot to jump out at us from behind a curtain.

CHAPTER 14

CALL TO THE NORTH

TORONTO

Meanwhile the call finally came to consider Little Trinity Church, Toronto, and I flew up for an interview, with Sandra following soon after. This very special parish met all our criteria plus, since it was in Canada, it meant that for all practical purposes I could put an international border between myself and FOCUS.

Little Trinity, the well-known nickname of a church whose official name was Trinity East, turned out to be a bustling urban parish with about 400 average Sunday attendance and a strong Evangelical Anglican tradition. I had known of the Church from others, and from the summer I served as a camp counselor at Ontario Pioneer Camp. I had also spoken on a couple of occasions to clergy groups in Canada. We prayed, and weighed all the options. Then we decided that this was indeed God's call.

Meanwhile FOCUS was going through a difficult period. Roger Dewey had been hired as Director, but was soon to be replaced by Woody Bowman. Each had tried to keep the ship afloat. But it nearly sank. During one of the dark periods, when donations had shrunk, and some even wondered if FOCUS had served its purpose, John Nicholson, a new Board Chair from Grosse Pointe, Michigan, helped clarify the vision and rouse the troops to continue with a firm commitment to keep FOCUS going.

Soon the board identified Simon Barnes as the likely new Director, and he took over the reins from Woody, who, to his immense credit, remained with FOCUS. When the time comes for his retirement Woody will have been the longest serving staffer in the organization. Soon the results of Simon's call were evident. With strong leadership gifts, he began to move the ministry forward. He proved to have remarkable fundraising abilities, and soon had the organization humming. During his years as Executive Director, which lasted until the end of 2002, the staff, budget, and especially facilities at the Study Center all saw marked growth.

CANADA SOJOURN

Meanwhile, I had arrived in Canada on April 1, 1986, dragging a trailer that contained books, a desk, and some clothes. The rest of the family would arrive later when the school year ended. Trekking across New York State in the direction of Niagara Falls, I wondered if I had made a terrible mistake. We were leaving behind almost everything that was familiar, and I was entering a new phase of life: a new job, a new city, a new country, a new neighborhood, and a new culture. I knew that Canada was definitely not the 51st state in the Union! This immense country had a culture and a history all its own, which meant that sermons peppered with quotes from Abraham Lincoln or *TIME* Magazine would simply not do. I also worried that, not having had a typical ministry, I might not be able to find enough ideas to fill weekly sermon after weekly sermon.

My fear was increased by a letter from Oliver O'Donovan. Oliver had been involved in FOCUS as a graduate student at Princeton and later rose to become Regis Professor of Moral Theology at Oxford. Oliver knew "Little" Trinity well, and wrote to me that he didn't know of any church in North America where people responded better to expository preaching than at Little "T." This not only whetted my appetite, but also increased my anxiety. Did I have what it takes?

I remember rising on the morning of April 1 to read my Bible in some motel in the middle of New York State. The passage assigned for that day in my Scripture Union notes was the Feeding of the Five Thousand. I read how Jesus took the small supply of bread and fish and multiplied it in abundance. As I meditated on this story I realized that God was asking me to count on him to do the same with my meager offerings. My job was to be faithful and offer him the best I could, and trust him to multiply it and feed his people.

Of all family members, Jennifer was the least happy with our decision. I ached for her. It meant leaving a school she enjoyed, and saying good-bye to close friends. She also had no experience of being the daughter of a parish rector, and soon resented some of the typical expectations that unwise parishioners laid on her. Her grief was real, with the consequence that those critical teenaged years in Canada led to a firm dislike of the country.

Kate had been born during our sojourn in Stamford. She continued to be a wide-eyed and wondering young girl: loving, fun, pixyish and beguiling. She endeared herself to everyone, especially her teachers. Although she and Jen had their moments, and she quickly learned the word "binoxous" as applied to an older sister, they were obviously fast friends. She, too, hated to leave Greenwich Academy. But, ever adaptable, Kate soon made friends in Canada, and became something of a model student.

Both Jen and Kate loved our delightful house on Plymbridge Road as I did. It was a Cape Cod styled brick house with virtually every modern convenience. Thankfully, it faced south and therefore caught all the winter sunshine that streamed through its abundant windows and sliding glass doors. It had a picturesque sunroom over which I grew morning glories in the summers. It looked over to a small river that wafted gurgling sounds into the backyard and gave us a pleasant vista across to pretty spaces on the other side. Best of all, from my point of view, it had a carpeted basement that became my study. We outfitted it with abundant built-in bookshelves to hold my growing library and furniture to accommodate small meetings. Even the trampoline that we had given Jen one Christmas in Stamford fitted nicely into a niche right behind the garage.

ILLNESS

Unfortunately, for Sandra, our Canadian sojourn was a period of protracted struggle with CFS, Chronic Fatigue Syndrome. This led to many days and weeks at home in bed, and to innumerable visits to doctors most of who didn't yet seem to understand the disease at all. Fortunately our bed in the master bedroom looked out on a very large picture window to the backyard and the river below provided a sylvan landscape for our homebound "invalid."

There were many things that made the decade we lived in Canada particularly satisfying to me. First, and most importantly, we were forced to rely on our own resources as a family as never before. We simply had no one else to turn to. Since all our friends and family were back in the States, we in effect circled the wagons, and drew closer to one another. Among the many memories I cherish were the late summer "daddy-daughter" camping trips with Jen and Kate.

Given my ineptitude at rural camping, these provided the three of us with lots of laughter and stories with which the girls could tease me. I also continued my practice of making up a bedtime saga for each child. These serial wonders began with the "Perils of Pauline" for Jen, when she was young. Pauline, loosely based on the main character in a pre-talkie movie by the same name, was always jumping from trains or lassoing criminals from the backs of horses. For Kate I created "Howda-Hooda"—another saga again loosely based on a cartoon character in the early years of TV. Finally for David, our newly-arrived son, I created "Snoop." Snoop was a hunchback do-gooder who ran a home for homeless street kids in Rio de Janeiro. David got particularly excited by the fact that in Snoop's dormitory where the kids were housed there was a trap door which provided escape from various predators.

We also had the incalculable benefit of a once-a-year Spring break trip to visit the children's grandparents in Hobe Sound, Florida. This annual escape from Toronto's long and often brutal winters was a marvelous tonic for us all, especially since we would invariably return in late March or early April to more cold! Beginning in January, perhaps Lent, Kate would create a wall calendar with palm trees for each day. Each day would then be marked off until finally we got to fly to "paradise."

UNEXPECTED PREGNANCY

In our second year in Toronto Sandra informed me that she was pregnant. Pregnant? I was nearly 52, and she 44. But, the surprising thing happened, and on September 13th, 1987, David Clark Moore was born in the Toronto General Hospital. This led to a sudden migration of cribs, bassinettes, diapers and baby paraphernalia that we thought had long vanished from our lives. But David was soon to make his presence felt, and what an incredible blessing he became. Someone quipped: "Well you have just decided to have your own grandchild!" David instantly captured our hearts, just as Jen and Kate had before. We were suddenly 5, and an added benefit in the eyes of our parishioners was the fact that we had a Canadian son.

Our small den, adjacent to the kitchen, was now augmented by a small slide. Also, we discovered that LEGO became a huge hit, because David manifested very early on a deep interest in construction. Houses would suddenly appear in his bedroom, created out of boxes that he had gathered. A local handyman took a real interest in David and built him an imaginative tree house in our back yard.

Jen continued to pursue her interest in ballet and became quite proficient at it. Kate parlayed her fascination with horses into a brief appearance in a made-for-TV movie where the young actress didn't know how to ride. With her beloved pony, Rusty, she began to rake in the blue ribbons at various shows. We amused ourselves with trips to Canada's Wonderland (a high quality amusement park), to Canada Place (a permanent exhibition with abundant hands-on activities for children), and the occasional dinner out. We celebrated twice in the restaurant on top of the CN Tower—the largest freestanding tower in the world. We nicknamed it the revolting restaurant because the food didn't quite match the view.

Toronto, in fact, was filled with fantastic things to do, and great places to eat. One restaurant quite near to where we lived, was a run by the famed Movenpick chain. It had a maze of fascinating food stations, leading us to eat many a Sunday lunch there. Also I needed access to good tennis and the children needed access to a pool, so we joined the nearby Toronto Cricket Club. Sandra's ministry was very one-on-one. But it included a vision to welcome the whole parish in shifts to Sunday afternoon teas at our house. Somewhere she found the most chochlatey cake I have ever tasted. She also continued to work on her art.

PARISH LIFE

Little Trinity was a unique parish. It had a strong missionary history and relished its Irish Protestant heritage. Its motto, proudly displayed on the Church's notice board outside, was "Holding forth the Word of Life." The interior of the Church was bare, though the exterior architecture was a beautiful expression of the Gothic Revival. It was the oldest surviving church building in Toronto, and boasted nearly 150 years of continuous worship—quite a long period for a relatively young country. To American Episcopalians the lack of candles, crosses, choir, vestments, and liturgical embellishments would seem strange. But, as one former rector put it: "Little Trinity has a meaningful absence of intended symbolism." Indeed, it combined being a Word-centered church with a strong emphasis on the Holy Communion. There was no need for a choir because the congregation sang both loudly and beautifully. Often I could hear parishioners singing in harmony.

For several years the church had embraced small groups. When I arrived, there were about 20 of them. They met in homes, were co-ed, multi-generational, and focused on Bible study, extempore prayer, and sharing of personal concerns. From a pastor's viewpoint, this was a huge gift. It meant that I could count on pastoral "first aid" being practiced in these groups, and I could also preach sermon series, while assigning the groups to study the same texts from the Bible on which I had preached. I soon began preaching a variety of sermon series, and eventually turned two of these into books: *One Lord, One*

Faith (based on the Apostles' Creed) and *A Church To Believe In* (a rudimentary ecclesiology that traced some specifically biblical and Anglican themes). Both books have seen second (revised) editions, and are still in print as I write some 20 years later. I am particularly thankful that these books have been widely used in churches across North America to further adult education.

I had begun my first book, *Disarming The Secular Gods*, during my pre-Toronto sabbatical year as part of a Doctor of Ministry program I undertook at Fuller Seminary. It awaits revision, but is still read and studied by select individuals and groups. With a Doctor of Ministry soon awarded by Fuller Seminary, and a parish graciously willing to release me to speak elsewhere, I found myself speaking and preaching across Canada and even in the States. I made frequent trips to places like Charleston, South Carolina, and other strongholds of orthodox and evangelical Anglicanism. I also wrote booklets and articles and made videos that were published by Inter-Varsity, Episcopalians United, Forward Movement, and the Bible Reading Fellowship.

Being the rector of what might arguably have been dubbed the Anglican Church of Canada's flagship evangelical parish, meant that my voice was heard. After having poured my energies primarily into youth, I was gratified to find that adults across the Continent were listening too. I firmly believe that it was neither eloquence nor brilliance that earned me these invitations. Many others were and are more skilled in speaking than I. But I believe I gained a hearing because I was uncompromising in proclaiming the Gospel and stood firmly on the authority of Scripture. Perhaps also being an American living in Canada made me something of a curiosity.

THEOLOGICAL CONTROVERSIES

The Anglican Church of Canada was facing the same issues that were bedeviling the Episcopal Church south of the border: homosexuality, theological pluralism, cultural compromise, and a rejection of Biblical authority. While Little Trinity cared for those caught in same-sex attraction, and even sought as a parish to be a base where such people could find pastoral help, it was united as a congregation the conviction that God could not bless same-sex relationships. That conviction was rooted not only in a high view of the Bible, but also in a concern for those who were seeking freedom from sexual compulsions. One such person, named Bill, came to me and revealed his dilemma. He had been trapped in a homosexual lifestyle for years and through a friend had been exposed to the Gospel. Yes, he wanted out; but more important, he wanted to find Christ. Bill did find Christ in the fellowship of Little Trinity, and eventually married a wonderful Christian woman in the parish. Together they witnessed both silently and openly to the grace of God in their lives.

Partly to stem the onward march of revisionist theology and ethics, I decided Canada needed a movement called Fidelity. This would be an answer to the well-established pro-gay movement named Integrity. Despite Fidelity's attempt to be objective, academic and pastorally sensitive it drew the ire of the gay community, which picketed its first conference. Nevertheless, ploughing ahead, it produced literature, and was even credited—by a Canadian bishop—with stemming the tide of the Church's rush towards the new "Gospel" of indiscriminate inclusivity.

My growing visibility in Canada, as a spokesperson for a classical Christian ethic regarding sexuality and marriage, led to an invitation to appear on "Good Morning Canada." This was not my first foray into the heady world of TV. My first TV appearance was during my early days with C.R.I.S. I auditioned and was given a spot on the show called "Password". There I promptly won $250, which was "real money" in those days, and if you can believe it, 1/10 of my annual salary. I had also appeared once on the Chicago Sunday Evening Club, a mainstream TV event that drew many popular preachers. I was disappointed in my own performance that evening, although a FOCUS trustee, Bill Kiesewetter, happened to catch the program and was graciously complimentary.

On Good Morning Canada I was invited to present the classical Christian ethic regarding sexuality. The other guest was Jim Ferry, an Anglican priest who had come out of the closet as an active homosexual and who was engaged in legal action with the Diocese of Toronto. In fact, he was suing both the Diocese and its bishop. Since I had no training how to function on a TV talk show, I spent the night sweating over books and notes in an effort to imagine the deep questions the moderator might ask me. As it turned out, he lobbed all the easy questions to the Rev. Ferry, giving him plenty of time to answer, and then tossed me a few red herrings. The show was obviously rigged to highlight the controversial and newsworthy aspects of this stormy controversy. I learned from that experience to come to a TV appearance prepared with whatever sound bytes I wanted to say, and if necessary to turn the questions around in order to get my licks in.

ANGLICAN ESSENTIALS

A highlight of my Canada years was my participation in the Essentials movement. Essentials began as a conference in 1994 in Montreal. Over 700 delegates from all across Canada arrived for the 5-day event that took place amid stiflingly hot and humid weather. In fact, the air conditioners condensed the steamy atmosphere into rain—inside the building! The conference produced the *Montreal Declaration*, and sparked a series of follow up conferences that presented the orthodox, evangelical, Anglican essentials in a way that was relevant to all the issues that were facing us. Essentials became a rallying cry for those who wanted to combine historic biblical faith with progressive methods of church life and witness.

My chapter in *Anglican Essentials,* the book that came out of the conference, was entitled "And Such Were Some of You." This proved to be perhaps the most controversial chapter because it critiqued the pro-gay position, and made a case for biblical sexuality. I had sweated over the chapter, and still think it was one of the most thoughtful pieces of writing I ever did. Perhaps my Canadian confreres asked me to address this hot topic, knowing that I could weather the criticism if it ever came, which it did. Actually, my paper made me something of a point man on the subject, and—together with Elaine Pountney, wife of Wycliffe College's then Principal Michael Pountney—I gave a series of addresses across Canada on sexuality. On three of these occasions, I was assigned bodyguards in case violence erupted.

Within the parish, I was concerned to motivate more men to take an active part in leadership and so began a men's ministry. We kicked it off with a luncheon at a downtown restaurant where I chided the 50 or so men who came by quoting a survey in *MacLean's* Magazine—Canada's answer to TIME. The survey asked readers to: "Finish this sentence: 'As Canadian as…'". In the States the answer would be easy: "As American as apple pie", or perhaps "As American as baseball". But in Canada where regional and linguistic differences are stressed, and where multiculturalism is the reigning social philosophy, the answer was not so easy. The Quebecois frequently threatened to separate their province from the rest, and resource-rich Western provinces resented the subsidies they paid to the poorer Eastern provinces. The answer that won, according to MacLean's was: "As Canadian as possible under the circumstances." This drew a laugh from the men, and we were off and running.

A fine men's ministry developed out of this venture, including a mid-winter "men's ski break." A group of seven or eight men, mostly businessmen and lawyers, left with me for a weekend of skiing at Mt. Tremblant in the Laurentians. We combined culinary exploits with Bible study and courageous efforts to ski in the bitter winter conditions. The weekend proved to be such fun that the same group with additions and subtractions continued the pattern for years to come. We migrated to the warmer climates of British Columbia after a few years, and then after a decade or so there to Vail, Colorado, where a dear friend, Joan Francis, lent her house to us year after year. I remember noting at one point that virtually all the men in the group had gone on to take active parts in the leadership either of Little Trinity or other parishes to which they transferred.

MISUNDERSTANDINGS AND STRUGGLES

My decade in Toronto was by no means the proverbial bunch of roses. There were conflicts in the parish—and not just over issues of sexuality where, thankfully, our entire congregation pretty much differed from the revisionist viewpoint of the denomination to which we belonged. The internal controversy surrounded what came to be known as the "Base Group Issue." Prior to my arrival at Little Trinity, a group of lay people in the parish, with the support of my predecessor, Fred Crook, came to the conclusion that the parish needed to offer a sizeable portion of its valuable downtown property to provide low and medium-cost housing to those who were increasingly being pushed out of the housing market because of rising real estate prices. A large building was contemplated, funded primarily by the Province of Ontario. By the time I arrived in 1986, the congregation was well on its way to moving forward with the plan. A group of laypeople who called themselves the "Base Group", led by Carla Cassidy, the former Rector's Warden, were promoting this course of action. From the moment of my arrival, they lobbied to enlist my support.

Initially, I was sympathetic. But a number of factors made me hesitate. Little Trinity had a unique heritage. It was one of the last remaining orthodox Anglican Evangelical parishes in the downtown area—if not *the* last. Its property, although not then in a particularly desirable area of the city, nevertheless had great value. I wondered if the time might not come when it was needed for church expansion. There were other reasons why the push for this program gave me pause. For one, we were giving away the property to the Government of Ontario. For another, since a secular entity (the Province) was in effect the developer, the parish would have no control over who lived in the building nor would it have unimpeded access to the residents once it was completed. To complicate matters, the proposed building would be physically joined to the Church itself.

Because we saw ourselves as a "congregationally-oriented" parish, the Base Group, which actually included several of my strong supporters, insisted that the matter should be put to a congregational vote. But, according to our diocesan canons, no property proposal could proceed to a congregational vote without the Rector's support. To bring it to a vote without the Rector's support would, in effect, create a referendum on his leadership. Therefore, with the full support of the vestry as well as the local bishop, we killed the plan. It was not put up for a vote.

This led to some very hard feelings. I recall that the tension was so strong on one occasion prior to our decision that I left a meeting in tears. On another occasion, a former rector quietly advised me to resign. But I stayed the course, and we worked through a reconciliation process created by the Mennonites that might well be a model for other congregations caught in similar conflicts. Thanks also to the help of Michael and Rosemary Green, who led our parish weekend with great wisdom and sensitivity that year, we reached an accommodation. For the next eight years of my tenure I felt that the peace of Christ had descended on us and the congregation flourished and grew.

Since this was my first and only parish rectorship, I was enormously grateful for the solid lay leadership that gathered around me. Not only were my wardens and vestry an excellent and faithful group to work with, but some of them, especially Doug and Ruth Grant and Liz Austin, were unusually prayerful and helpful, as was Stony Robinson and Doug Milloy. Doug Grant, president of a local investment company and Ruth, a board member of several important Toronto institutions, became heart-and-soul leaders in the congregation. They were always fun to be with, and Ruth was an avid tennis player, who beat me on one occasion—to the delight of everyone! Together with my "ski buddies," most of whom were beginning to exercise leadership in one way or another, I had a strong phalanx of supporters with whom to pray, strategize, and steer the congregation in healthful ways. I should also mention Duke Vipperman, my trusted Associate Rector. Duke was not only a good preacher, but an excellent pastor. He and I worked well together, and together with Margaret Morgan, our staunch and spiritually sensitive parish secretary, we made a united and smooth-working team.

FAMILY JOURNEYS

Back home in our quiet valley nicknamed "Hoggs Hollow," the family also flourished. Jen went off to Johns Hopkins College to pursue undergraduate education, and dutifully returned to Toronto each summer to get local jobs and to stay close to the family. It meant a great deal to me that she would return and be with us during our Canadian sojourn. Kate continued at St. Clement's, the nearby girls' private school to which both she and Jen had gone. Despite inadequacies, especially in its preparation for entrance to American universities, St. Clement's proved to be a good school for them. One of my greatest joys during those years was having breakfast with Kate each morning in our sunroom. These times included Bible reading and prayer. I could sense that she had a warm and genuinely open attitude towards God, and as a consequence we drew close together spiritually

David meanwhile grew into a sturdy little kid, inventive, resourceful, and with a strong connection to Sandra. I struggled to be a good dad to him; but only later truly bonded thanks to a series of father/son adventures we started taking each year.

I tended a flower garden that we planted. It relished the cool summer months, adding color and decoration to our attractive house. We took off for the States (as we came to call the U.S.A.—following Canadian custom) as often as we could. In addition to our Spring Break jaunts to Florida, during my summer vacations we would zoom off to Boston, Cape Cod, Nantucket, or Martha's Vineyard. In the few days I took off after Christmas, we crossed the border into Vermont for some family skiing at Stowe. One regret I have is that we did not take advantage as much as I would have liked of the endless summer activities Canada had to offer: The Muskoka Lakes region, The Shaw Festival in Niagara-on-the-Lake, and the

Shakespeare Festival in Stratford, Ontario. But we had at least a small taste of each.

Of particular importance to me during this decade (1985-95) was the opportunity to write. I had written innumerable fund-raising letters for C.R.I.S. and FOCUS, but in Toronto I discovered that I had a message to get out through articles and books. My various sermon series provided the raw material for future chapters. Plus I was enormously helped by a gifted editor in the parish, Denyse O'Leary. I find it interesting that all three of the major books I've written were published while I was rector of Little Trinity. It fulfills the old adage: "If you want to get something done, find the busiest person and then get them to do it." I was gratified when many members of the congregation gobbled these books up, even if only as memorabilia. I was equally disappointed that FOCUS made so little use of them. FOCUS seemed to want me as a figurehead and fundraiser, but not as a speaker or teacher. For example, I was invited and then disinvited to speak at a major FOCUS conference. This was particularly painful. Having spoken in so many school chapels to eager audiences, I knew I could connect with teens. But if truth be told, FOCUS probably needed me more as a *pater familias* than as a speaker or teacher.

What did become clear from our Canadian sojourn was that I now had a totally new life that was branching out in quite different directions. Our vibrant youth ministry at Little Trinity was in the capable hands of young couples, so I was left to expend my energies on those who were at least somewhat closer to my own age. I wrote a steady stream of articles on all sorts of subjects that were published in *Christian Week*, an interdenominational Canadian newspaper, as well as in other publications. In the years to come, I realized that all this writing and speaking was preparing me for my future role as seminary dean. Without that prior experience, I might not have been prepared for the challenges that lay ahead.

FAR AWAY TRAVELS

Before I leave my reminiscences of Canada, three incidents should be mentioned. The first was a rare opportunity to travel to South Africa. For many years I had retained the position of North American "Secretary" for the worldwide Evangelical Fellowship in the Anglican Communion. EFAC's work in North America in some ways paled by comparison with a series of excellent Theological Round-Tables that the British EFAC sponsored in the Third World. Being invited to participate in these afforded me the opportunity to visit Jamaica, Nigeria, and South Africa. Papers I contributed became chapters in books published by EFAC. The trip to South Africa was particularly noteworthy, because it also included my only foray so far to Asia. With a mere 100,000 accrued "air miles," Air Canada allowed me to fly to Johannesburg via Anchorage and Hong Kong. The trip was not only completely free, but it was first class all the way. While in Hong Kong I stayed with friends from Little Trinity who had moved there.

After the Round Table in Johannesburg, I spent a long weekend in Cape Town visiting friends from the past who were now living there—one of whom was an economically-challenged professor and his wife at the University of Cape Town. The other, an old friend from my student days in England, was the son of a famous South African polo player. His family estate turned out to be one of the great old Dutch plantations of the Cape Province. Through him, and through a visit to Soweto, I gained a fresh understanding of the struggle to end apartheid, and both the hopes and risks ahead for the new South Africa.

It was a startling experience to stand right at the Cape of Good Hope, the confluence of the Atlantic and Indian Oceans. I couldn't help but think about the many great ships that had passed that legendary promontory over the centuries. My visit to South Africa fortunately also included a long weekend at Kruger National Park where, thanks to a skilled guide, I saw virtually every wild animal of the area in its natural setting. I was particularly awed by the wild dogs that kill by pulling their victims apart with their teeth. The pack was a mere 100 yards away.

An amusing incident happened in Jamaica on the conclusion of our Round Table there. A British bishop and I decided to spend an afternoon at Ochos Rios, a delightful beach at the bottom of Dunns River Falls—a major tourist attraction. While I sat on the beach, my bishop friend took off for a swim. Before I knew what had happened, a very attractive young Jamaican woman bounded up to me, sat down and snuggled right up. Rather than rudely shoo her off, I decided to engage her in conversation—making sure she knew that I was happily married with a wife and children roughly her age. That seemed to make no difference to her. When the proper British bishop returned to see this chatty twosome sitting close together on the sand, he wisely said nothing. Soon another nubile Jamaican bounded up to him and sat down. He played along with the game as best he could. Finally the two women left, and as we climbed up the Falls to our parked car, we saw them picnicking with a bunch of twenty something friends. They waved at us and said friendly goodbyes using our names. In retrospect, the only sense I can make of the bizarre occasion was that the women must have been acting on a dare.

Two other events must be mentioned. The first was the surprise visit of none other than Mother Theresa to our offices at Little Trinity. The world-famous nun from Albania and Calcutta wandered in one afternoon, looking for a building in which to house an AIDS hospice she was hoping to start in Toronto. Seeing the two derelict buildings at the edge of our property, she and my secretary chatted about whether they might be put to good use. It was my bad luck to be out of the office that afternoon, and the little lady in the white habit never returned.

The other event was equally disappointing. Prince Charles and Princess Diana of England were visiting Toronto on the royal yacht *Britannia*, and sought an Anglican Church in which to worship on the Sunday morning. Since we were celebrating our 150th anniversary, worshipped in one of the City's most historic buildings, and were conveniently located downtown, the tentative plan was for them to come to us on Sunday. But the visit was not to be. Less than a month before the appointed day, a bus appeared, carrying the Prince's secretary and a retinue of well-dressed assistants. Looking around at our rather plain interior, which featured none of the usual trappings to be found in Anglican churches, the Prince's secretary asked me: "Well, padre, how long do you usually preach?" "Oh, about twenty minutes", I said. "Twenty minutes? You certainly give the people their money's worth." The next day, the royal visit was moved to the Cathedral down the road, where the Prince and Princess endured no more than an eight-minute homily.

CHAPTER 15

TRINITY SEMINARY

THE CALL TO RETURN

David was born when Sandra was forty-four and I fifty-two. I was worried that, with a baby coming so late in our lives, there might be physical complications. But, try as I might, I was unsuccessful in getting special health insurance in the States on the off-chance that David would be born with some disability, and we decided to return. Thankfully, my fears proved unfounded, and David was perfectly healthy. However, this concern did get me thinking that, as I approached my sixtieth year, it would be foolish to wait much longer in Canada because my age might lessen the chances of employment back in the States. Still full of energy, and feeling that I had many more years of ministry left in me, I was eager to sink my teeth into to a new challenge.

That challenge came in the form of a surprising and extremely welcome call to become the fourth Dean and President of Trinity Episcopal School for Ministry. I had not only been the School's first Chairman of the Board, and one of its founders, but during our Canadian sojourn I had remained on the Board. Also, I had taught several courses for Trinity during its winter and summer Inter-terms. Even though I only had a Doctor of Ministry and not the preferred Ph.D., my decade of parish experience coupled with the books I had published qualified me for serious consideration. Later, I was told that after the Board consulted John Stott and J.I. Packer, and received strong endorsements, they made their move. I was duly interviewed and in the end was chosen from among three finalists. We sold our Canadian house, and on December 31, picked up stakes and moved to a new home in Western Pennsylvania.

Our move coincided with the decade's worst blizzard. The morning after, Kate and I donned cross-country skis and slid around the neighborhood before the plows came. We were soon acclimatizing ourselves to our new surroundings in the Pittsburgh area, where I had lived during my very first parish appointment. We all thought our new home truly beautiful. Sandra and I had each selected it on separate scouting visits—each without telling the other. The house was large enough to accommodate the four of us—with a bedroom for Jen when she returned home from college. It could also welcome large groups of faculty, students and trustees for the innumerable social events that being head of a graduate institution requires. There would be three annual parties for trustees and faculty, all of whom fitted into our living and dining room on couches or folding chairs—sometimes 50-60 strong. These evenings were more than social occasions, though they included good food and wine. After dessert, we would have a visiting speaker who talked informally on some aspect of global church life. Many internationally known bishops and theologians trooped through during those Trinity years, and 606 East Drive served us well both as an official residence and also as a real home.

My study was in a small south wing that sprouted off the living room. It was fitted with endless bookshelves that, together with those that lined the living room, accommodated my burgeoning library. (When we eventually left Pennsylvania in 2008, I divested myself of half of that library.) In addition to my study, some of the nicest features of the house were its enchanting kitchen, immense basement, and a charming back yard that included an ample patio. I tended a garden in one of the far corners of the yard, and we found space for games of bocce ball, baseball, mini-golf, lacrosse, a trampoline, and even croquet. The yard made it possible, in addition to the many faculty and trustee gatherings, for Sandra to have student moms with their little ones over to play. Plus we had an annual all-school picnic there, and large birthday parties too.

SEWICKLEY

Adjustment to nearby Sewickley Academy proved to be difficult, especially for David. He found a not-very-friendly group of classmates that made his transfer in the middle of the school year painful. I remember being quite angry at the way some of the kids were treating him and had to restrain myself from taking inappropriate action.

In time, David made his peace with his classmates, and all the boys in the class would come to a series of birthday parties each September. These parties enhanced his image and, in addition to food and on-site games, included an annual birthday car rally. This adventure put Trinity students behind the wheels as drivers, and took the boys all around the area on a mysterious circuit in search of answers to printed clues.

I made these clues as mischievous as possible. For example, on one occasion, the boys had to "beg" ice cream from a roadside merchant. They were not allowed to pay, and the merchants were in on the fun. They had promised to give the boys a hard time, even though the ice cream had been paid for in advance. Eventually, of course, the merchants gave in.

We made our church home at St. Stephen's, a large, biblically-grounded congregation just down the road. Basking in the glow of John Guest's noteworthy ministry there, but now under the capable new leadership of Geoff Chapman, this parish had become a leading light in the struggle for theological orthodoxy and Gospel-centered spirituality throughout the Episcopal Church. I was frequently away on weekends, preaching here and there, so we faced a challenge integrating our family at St. Stephen's. Because I was the Dean of Trinity, my attendance there always felt semi-official. David also struggled to fit into the youth group, and eventually found fellowship at another church group in the area. Kate, on the other hand, did find friends at St. Stephen's, and one particular friend, Sean Norris. After a mission trip to Central America with the youth group, she returned with the handsome Sewickley soccer hero in tow. They became a pair virtually from that moment on. To our immense joy, they married as soon as Kate finished college.

Being Dean of the Episcopal Church's only evangelical seminary was fascinating. One challenge was our tenuous relationship to the institution that we sought to serve and influence. Trinity had been founded in the burst of new life that appeared in many of the mainline Protestant denominations during the 1960s and 1970s. This movement was evangelical at first, and then gracefully charismatic, as people hungry for spiritual vitality discovered the gifts of the Spirit.

Out of this new life came a growing crop of men and women seeking ordination. In this burst of enthusiasm, Trinity was born.

RENEWAL IN A MAINLINE DENOMINATION

But, of course, the question arises: why was Trinity Seminary formed in the first place? After all, there were already 10 seminaries serving the relatively small Episcopal Church, and a couple of them had been formed by merging struggling ones. Was there really a need for yet another?

To explain our need requires a quick overview of the history of our denomination in the United States. Episcopalians were, at first, just the Church of England in the American colonies. Then, following the Revolutionary War, we separated from the Church of England and became the Episcopal Church.

Following a period of spiritual dryness in the late 18th century, the Episcopal Church began to grow and prosper during the early 19th century. The driving force of that growth and renewal within the church was evangelical. This evangelical movement was dynamic, life-giving, and fiercely Protestant. Eventually it would be characterized as "Low Church" in ethos and conservative in theology.

Not all Episcopalians were enamored of this new life, and a counter-movement was formed that took its inspiration from England's Catholic-inspired Oxford Movement. Tensions developed between the two wings of the new Episcopal Church, prompting the withdrawal of the Reformed Episcopal Church in 1873 over ritualistic practices that had begun to creep in.

The Low Church/Evangelical movement reached its high water mark under the influence of Phillips Brooks, the enormously attractive (and magisterial) Rector of Trinity Church, Boston, and later bishop of Massachusetts.

Brooks, it turned out however, was more influenced by the inroads of higher criticism of the Bible and the waves of liberal thought than many of his Low Church colleagues realized. Over time he had become dissatisfied with what he saw as the insular and backward-looking evangelicalism of his roots, and especially the pietistic training he had received at Virginia Seminary. Under his leadership, what came to be known as the "Broad Church" party (moderate in churchmanship, liberal in theology) began to grow in prominence. Evangelicalism, now tainted by association with the "schismatic" Reformed Episcopalians, and tarred with the brush of Fundamentalism in the minds of academia, receded into the dim past.

For the first half of the 20th century, Episcopal evangelicalism, with its emphasis on evangelism, lay witness, small group Bible study, extempore prayer, and heart-felt piety, was almost forgotten. Churches prospered, buildings sprouted up, numbers climbed—especially as the Episcopal Church was caught up in the post-World War II boom in attendance and church construction.

But by the late 1950s and early 1960s there were new stirrings that saw the emergence of a new evangelicalism in all the mainline Protestant churches, including the Episcopal Church. A good deal of this, I believe, was thanks to the impact of Billy Graham's crusades that reached across all denominational lines and introduced many lay people to a fresh experience of Jesus Christ.

EARLY STIRRINGS

Even prior to Billy Graham's historic ministry, I recall an amazing mission held in the late 1940s at New York's Cathedral of St. John the Divine. A British evangelist named Bryan Green preached the Gospel effectively to busloads of Episcopalians who streamed into Manhattan's upper West Side. As I recall the event, being all of 11 or 12 years old, I think it was the first time I had heard the Gospel clearly preached by someone wearing a clerical collar.

Sparked by these missions and crusades, Episcopalians began to wake up to the richness of their own heritage. A series of organizations sprung up, beginning with the Fellowship Of Witness, which I helped to start, with the guiding hand of Philip Hughes who, along with Stuart Babbage, had migrated to Georgia as theological faculty. Hughes was from South Africa, and Babbage was an Australian. Both were gifted scholars steeped in the tradition of British Anglican Evangelicalism. Hughes later moved to Philadelphia, and took a chair teaching theology at Westminster Seminary.

Other organizations such as Faith at Work were founded. Originally the vision of Sam Shoemaker, the dynamic and controversial rector of Calvary Church, Pittsburgh, Faith at Work spearheaded a Gospel thrust into the business community and also encouraged laity to share their experience of Christ in churches and informal settings. Then Faith Alive began to organize teams of laity to visit churches and pass on the fire of new life in Christ.

By the early 60s we saw the emergence of the charismatic movement. Inspired by the outbreak of *glossolalia* that had appeared much earlier in the 20th century in Los Angeles, this new emphasis was on spiritual gifts, and it swept many nominal Episcopalians into renewal. Places like Houston's Church of the Redeemer with its remarkable gifting in contemporary liturgical music and community life, St. Luke's Church in Akron, and later St. Paul's Episcopal Church in Darien, Connecticut, drew hundreds, and then thousands, to "see what was happening." The Episcopal Charismatic Fellowship was one of several new organizations that sprang up as a result.

Soon, parishes all over the Episcopal Church, and even whole dioceses, were feeling the breath of the Holy Spirit in new and exciting ways—much to the consternation of traditionalists and liberals who couldn't for the life of them figure out what was happening.

In Pittsburgh, John Guest, an Englishman who had been working with Scripture Union, was called to be rector of the leading parish in the Diocese. Through him, St. Stephen's became one of the first parishes in the country to see dynamic growth with conversions on a weekly basis, undergirded by solid biblical preaching. Other churches in the Diocese of Pittsburgh caught fire, some leaning more in the charismatic direction like St. Martin's, Monroeville. Then in 1981, Alden Hathaway, a former seminary classmate of mine, was elected sixth bishop of Pittsburgh. Enormously gifted as a preacher of the Gospel, passionately committed to mission and evangelism, Hathaway began to turn the diocese around from the bonhomie of cocktail party schmoozing clergy I recall from my years there in 1961-1963 into a powerhouse for the Gospel.

FOUNDING TRINITY

Alden Hathaway and Jim Hampson, another seminary friend, had gone to one of their professors back in 1961 when we were all students together. They asked the Old Testament professor, Harvey Guthrie: "What's with this Peter Moore? He seems different. He seems to take the Bible at face value." Guthrie assured these two young seminarians that "Peter Moore represents a kind of German pietism that has nothing to do with the Episcopal Church." That settled the issue for them at the time until—faced with the bankruptcy of their early ministries—both fell flat on their faces before the Lord and were soundly born again. Hathaway and Hampson put their considerable energies into assisting with the creation and establishment of Trinity School for Ministry, or Trinity Episcopal School for Ministry, as it was then called.

Soon, both popular and scholarly-minded Episcopalians began rallying in support of the new evangelical movement. Among them were Fitz Allison and John Rodgers, two gifted professors at Virginia Seminary. When they allied themselves with the newly created Trinity Seminary, people looked up and took notice.

I vividly recall the first National Episcopal Conference on Evangelism, held at St. Phillip's Cathedral in Atlanta some time around 1974. I had been invited as a speaker. At a pregnant moment when John Guest and I rose to announce to the 1000 participants that we were going to start a new, evangelical seminary, you'd have thought Vesuvius had erupted. A two-minute standing ovation followed, revealing to us just how needed such an institution was. John Guest and I had already visited the Presiding Bishop, John M. Allin, and expressed our desire to start a new seminary. We received a lukewarm reception. We had also visited John Coburn, then President of the House of Clerical and Lay Deputies, and later Bishop of Massachusetts. He, too, had been very hesitant to encourage us. However, he did say: "Well, every movement in the Episcopal Church has started its own seminary, so I don't see any reason why yours shouldn't too." We took that as a green light. Later when I became the Fourth Dean, I received a surprisingly warm letter of congratulations from then Bishop Coburn, who had also been my Dean at E.T.S. when I studied there in 1961.

So it was that in 1976, Trinity opened its doors. Somehow I was pronounced the first Chairman of the board, and on that board I served for the next twenty years. By the time I became Dean/President in 1996, Trinity had become a well-established institution. However, despite the Seminary's impressive rise, it would be wrong to think that it was ever truly accepted by the whole Church. Throughout its foundational years, a majority of bishops refused to send us students, although in a curious twist, many of those same bishops did accept our graduates. I would like to think that was because they were impressed with their quality and commitment.

Trinity both reflected and fostered renewal within the Episcopal Church. Our first Dean/President, Bishop Alfred Stanway, a retired Australian who served for years in Tanzania, encouraged us not to worry about the lack of welcome. "Just go where you are welcomed, and trust God to open doors." Such was the influence of Trinity and various renewal ministries in Pittsburgh that by the time I returned to the Diocese in 1996 to be Dean of Trinity, Pittsburgh was an entirely different sort of place than I had left behind in 1963.

One of my first duties as the fourth Dean of Trinity was to attend the annual conference of deans of Episcopal seminaries. This three-day retreat for all the deans of Episcopal seminaries (now all eleven of us) was held at various locations around the country. As gatherings, they were polite, restrained, and filled with superficial chatter. We tinkered with institutional issues but rarely if ever ascended to the level of real theological discussion. Our starting points, as theologians, were simply too far apart. The closest the group came to a theological discussion was when we did some Bible study together. But apart from that, the atmosphere bordered on chilly and I felt that any encouraging news that I might share from Trinity was embarrassingly unwelcome. When our student numbers began to climb, and actually surpassed the largest of the other eleven seminaries for a few years, I began to feel downright uncomfortable. We were clearly a pariah in the eyes of this rarefied group of theological liberals. Only when Philip Turner was present, or later when Robert Munday was appointed Dean of Nashotah House, did I find people in this group with whom I could easily talk. On reflection, I think I should have tried harder, and my own defensiveness probably played a larger part than I was willing to admit at the time.

LIFE ON CAMPUS

As with the history of FOCUS, the history of Trinity's founding has been amply documented in Janet Leighton's book, *Lift High The Cross* (Harold Shaw, 1995). What I inherited in 1996 was a vibrant board of trustees and a faculty that had earned the respect of a generation or two of students. My immediate predecessor, Bill Frey, former Bishop of Colorado, had left a very deep impression—not only because his *basso profundo* voice sounded like God's on the Seminary's telephone answering machine, but also because he and his wife Barbara had deep faith and a profound commitment to renewal. He had left a legacy of spiritual renewal in Colorado that unfortunately was not to be continued by his successors. Some on our faculty and board were initially worried that my own mainline Evangelical theological point of view might make me unsympathetic to the charismatic strain that ran through Trinity's life at the time. But they had no need to worry. Sandra's and my years at St. Paul's, Darien, in the early Eighties had given us ample opportunity to appreciate the strengths of the charismatic movement while distancing ourselves from its more extreme elements.

I taught homiletics (preaching) to all second-year students each fall semester. This gave me a direct connection with each M.Div. student, and also provided me with a welcome classroom experience.

I discovered that classroom teaching was one of the most enjoyable aspects of ministry. The course I developed combined a theology of preaching with practical helps and I stressed that all preaching should be grounded in the gospel of grace. I discovered something that was later brought home by my successor at Trinity, Paul Zahl, namely that even among solidly converted students there was a tendency to rely on a *de facto* theology of "salvation by good works". This old bugaboo, sometimes called Pelagianism or semi-Pelagianism, was endemic within our denomination. People who were otherwise solidly evangelical in their theology would slip back into preaching sermons that were exhortations to "do more, try harder, be more spiritual" and so on. Few sermons took adequate account of the Pauline concept that even though Christ had fully accomplished our salvation through his Cross and Resurrection we always remained *simul justus et peccator* (both justified and yet still sinners).

RAISING FUNDS

Being the Dean of Trinity meant I had to do a lot of fund-raising. Trinity's budget required an annual infusion of donations to supplement its modest income from tuition. This stretched my faith and sent me to my knees. I came to the conclusion that, while my predecessor Deans Stanway, Rodgers, and Frey, seemed to have the "gift of faith" for money, I did not. Each June, as the end of our fiscal year approached and as potential deficits loomed on the horizon, I would become anxious and seek God in prayer. One year I recall being in tears. But God's faithfulness outshone my lack of faith. Out of eight years as Dean I can only recall two when we did not raise enough funds to cover expenses.

It soon became clear to me that we needed a capital campaign to beef up our tiny endowment and to upgrade our buildings, among other things. My years at FOCUS had equipped me to raise money, and so with the Board's encouragement, and a carefully planned feasibility study, we embarked on the *Such Faith Campaign* with a goal of raising $12 million. There is no way I would have done this without the amazing support of a solid phalanx of helpers, most notable among them being Peter Clark. Peter, Sandra's brother, had proved to be not only a trusted friend, but also an enormous support both with Trinity and with FOCUS, especially in the area of fundraising. George Gallup III, of the famed Gallup Poll family, who had also become a special friend, graciously accepted our invitation to be honorary chair of the Campaign.

What I had not factored in was the toll a major capital campaign would take on me personally, and on the family. Capital campaigns, especially in institutions where one cannot rely on wealthy alumni to ante up, require an amazing amount of travel. I logged in thousands of miles, chalked up an impressive tally of frequent flyer miles, and talked with endless potential donors. In the end, a few enormously generous donors pushed our results well over the $12 million mark.

We celebrated our goal with a large party at Trinity, and two years later when our new library/academic building was completed, we celebrated again with a visit from George Carey, the 103rd Archbishop of Canterbury. His presence on our campus was the occasion of great rejoicing, replete with an elegant English garden party, and—of course—lectures and panels. It was also, in many ways, Trinity's "coming out party" since we were one of the very few seminaries in the United States to have been visited by a sitting Archbishop of Canterbury. Lord Carey's evangelical sympathies were doubtless one of the reasons why he chose to be with us. But clearly he was fully aware that Trinity had been widely and unfairly discriminated against in the Episcopal Church. He seems to have thought it right to lay the wider church's stamp of approval on our efforts. His visit, and later my opportunity to speak at a pre-Lambeth conference for international bishops in 1996 in Canterbury, England, made me mutter to myself: "Well, I can die now. I've done the work I was meant to do." How wrong I was.

LEADING TOURS

Being a seminary Dean involves many duties. For one thing, my calendar was filled with speaking and preaching opportunities. Being one of the few conservative voices within the Episcopal Church thrust me into diocesan meetings, and even earned me a spot on the cover of *Episcopal Life*. If you add up all my travels with FOCUS, and C.R.I.S. before that, I believe I have visited every major city in the United States (including Hawaii and Alaska), most Caribbean countries, the bulk of Europe, Africa, the Middle East and South America.

A group called First Century Voyages, run by David Spence of Chapel Hill, NC, thought that I might be able to recruit people to go on some globe-trotting voyages where fun would be combined with spiritual nourishment. Perhaps that was in part because, prior to his invitation, I had led a bus trip from Geneva through Marseilles to Paris. Sponsored by Trinity, we traced the origins of the French Reformation. On this trip, we managed to include side trips to the famed monastery at Taize as well as a visit to Arles where Vincent Van Gogh painted some of his best work. Interestingly, a much later trek took us along a similar route, this time down the Rhone in a long, sleek riverboat with 30 people in tow.

But twice during this period, and once later, David Spence invited me to help lead cruises aboard the Sea Cloud. This legendary vessel, built for Marjorie Merriweather Post—the much-married millionairess who was once the richest woman in America—was now being chartered by his First Century Voyages company. I helped lead two tours on this luxury yacht, with staterooms that would suit a sultan. One trip was to Turkey and Greece, and focused on the fabled Seven Churches of Revelation. This combined a bus tour to Pergamum, Sardis, Smyrna, Ephesus, and the like with a cruise across the Aegean Sea stopping at exotic ports of call such as Patmos, Corinth, Athens, Thessalonika, Troas, and Istanbul. Imagine us celebrating Holy Communion at the very spring in Philippi where Paul began his European mission, and doing the same in the former palace of the Sultan of Istanbul! David asked me to lead a repeat of this tour in 2011 on the Sea Cloud II, with the bulk of people recruited from the Carolinas and Virginia. Having now visited the Greek port city of Corinth four times in my life, I am now satisfied to think that I know it.

The Sea Cloud tour in between these two happened immediately after the disastrous attack on the World Trade Towers in New York City and the Pentagon on September 11, 2001. Although half the tour group bowed out at the last minute, fearing to fly after skyjack terrorists had flown passenger planes into these buildings, the rest of us still toured Tuscany in Italy, the West Coast of Italy, and the Cote d'Azur in France. This time I helped give talks on famous Christians who had lived in this area, whose writings influenced Christian history: Augustine, Catherine of Sienna, Savonarola, Peter Waldo, Blaise Pascal, and so forth. My appreciation of fine cuisine, gracious hospitality, history and delightful conversation all combined to make these two tours extraordinary. Paul Zahl was my co-leader on the first tour, and Bill Edgar on the second. I refused to be embarrassed by the luxury of these voyages, realizing that the people who go on them will travel in style one way or another. But I was also wary of being seduced by the sheer opulence of it all.

ADMINISTRATION

I had several goals in my faculty appointments at Trinity. I wanted faculty who had distinguished themselves as exponents of classical Anglican evangelical thought. I also wanted to balance what I perceived to be a faculty composed mostly of strong introverts. Thirdly, I wanted a group of men (and women) who could equip students to preach and teach the Bible—including the Old Testament—from a fully Christ-centered point of view. With solid input from the faculty themselves, I found an excellent crop of new faculty. However, the turnover meant that I had to let one or two faculty go, whom I thought were not pulling their weight. Soon I discovered what all academic administrators eventually discover: Once you bring a faculty member on, that person can easily turn from being a friend or colleague to a potential adversary. This all-too-subtle shift is in part caused by the role the Dean/President must play as the point man for hirings, preferments, salaries, and other institutional relationships.

While I was very proud of the faculty that I inherited and gathered, one incident overshadows those eight years. Ever watchful over the financial state of the School, I realized in early January of 2003 that we were likely to fall short that fiscal year to the tune of $100,000. I had not faced a deficit like that since my first year as Dean, and it worried me sick. Taking counsel with my Academic Dean, Gavin McGrath, and my Dean of Operations, Wicks Stephens, the three of us agreed that if we could let one faculty member go at the end of that academic year, we could avoid what I saw as a financial disaster. The obvious person to be let go was Pam Powell. Pam was an ordained Presbyterian (UP-USA), and very likeable as well as faithful. But she had not received particularly strong marks in the student evaluation forms at the end of each semester, and her take-home pay was significantly augmented by teaching several inter-term courses on top of her regular load. We decided that the way to save $100,000 was to make 2003 Pam's last year with us.

Unfortunately, Pam was the only woman on the faculty and, if we let her go, Trinity might be vulnerable to the criticism (already voiced in some quarters) that we were unsupportive of women in ministry. Although my own stance in favor of women's ordination was well-known, our decision (which was shared with Pam) met with instant and vigorous disapproval. Various efforts were made to find "legal" reasons why I had not followed the Faculty Handbook, although the lawyers on the Board said that I had at least followed the "letter of the law." But the incident led to a rebellion on the part of the faculty. They circled the wagons and would not even talk as individuals to various Board members. Things got ugly, and for a time I felt I could not even join the faculty in prayer at our usual Friday morning meetings. Inwardly, I felt sick and betrayed, especially because Gavin McGrath, my Academic Dean, did a complete turnaround. Under pressure from other faculty, he switched his position, leaving me and my Administrative Assistant, Wicks Stephens, as the only ones in favor of the move.

On reflection, the faculty's concerns about letting the one and only woman on our faculty go were valid, even though it was my stated intention to seek another female faculty member when funding was restored. In the end, Steve Smith, a long-time faculty member, offered his resignation for health reasons, and the $100,000 package that I so needed was found. Pam remained on the faculty two more years. But the kerfuffle it all caused made me, at the age of 67, realize that to continue indefinitely as Dean and President was not a wise idea. I lost a great deal of my zeal for fundraising, and so tendered my resignation for the following year, planning on retiring in June of 2004.

In the providence and through the grace of God, the faculty managed to have what is often referred to as a "come to Jesus meeting". We reconciled, attributed good motives to each other, and vowed to move on. In a curious way, my final year, 2003-2004, proved to be my happiest. Relieved from the burden of seeking acceptance, and with a surprising financial grant to beautify the campus, I set about being chief decorator and landscape gardener. All sorts of beautification projects were completed that year, including a conference room in the Administration building that, because of its deep red wallpaper, the faculty affectionately dubbed the "bordello room". Curiously also, that final year was a time during which I drew personally close to a number of students. I was invited to join a small student fellowship group that met off-campus, and I became long-term friends with several of these students. The discovery that I was being called to a new role of mentoring younger men opened my eyes to a whole new phase of life.

Along with this went the realization that, organizationally speaking, my major life's work was complete. Now was a time to invest in the lives of others. I left Trinity in the Spring of 2005, thinking at 68 that I had done my last job. Again, I was quite wrong. I had forgotten that the word "retirement" is nowhere to be found in the Bible!

CHAPTER 16

RETIREMENT?

FAUX RETIREMENT

My speaking and writing ministry continued, having greatly expanded throughout the eight years of my tenure at Trinity. For example, I would preach annually at St. Phillips, Charleston thanks to Jim Hampson's gracious invitations. I would also take parish weekends, and was invited to preach occasionally as well. Several dioceses asked me to speak on the conservative side of the theological wars that were heating up on issues such as theological pluralism, sexuality, and the authority of the Bible. I debated a revisionist priest who was taking the pro-gay side of the sexuality argument. My presentation became a booklet that was fairly widely distributed, and again catapulted me into the spotlight on that critical issue.

As the prospect of retirement from Trinity in 2004 loomed, I had no clear direction for the future. I began to feel very uneasy. For one thing, Sandra had been spending longer and longer periods away from home. Much of this was her pursuit of the health-giving advice she received at a counseling center in Edmonds, Washington, I joined her there on several occasions, and was helped myself. Sandra was finally getting the support she needed for her life-long eating disorder, and she was eager learn how to share all that she was learning. So, with long periods at home alone, and yet still blessed with good health and boundless energy, I did not relish the prospect of retirement. Fortunately, retirement was not to be.

HELPING THE NEEDIEST

By 2004 I was turning 68, and had been in the ordained ministry since 1961—that is 44 years. But because I have always had a lot of energy, I was eager for a new challenge.

Three new ventures presented themselves, two of which appealed to my entrepreneurial side, and one to my wanderlust side. First there was the creation of the Anglican Relief and Development Fund (ARDF) in 2003. With the encouragement of Simon Barnes, who had moved from FOCUS to an organization called Geneva Global and with the support of Bishop Bob Duncan, then head of the so-called Network (of orthodox Anglicans), and Archbishop of the Anglican Church of North America, ARDF was formed. The aim was to raise money in North America for carefully researched, high-impact projects in the Two Thirds World that would also have a Gospel component. Geneva Global, a private foundation, would do the research and present the ARDF trustees with in-depth research. We would raise the money.

Half of the ARDF Board consisted of international Primates—that is, head bishops of the 38 Anglican Provinces worldwide. The Archbishops of the West Indies, Uganda, Kenya, Nigeria, Central Africa, and Southeast Asia all agreed to serve. Later the Archbishops of West Africa and Jerusalem, Egypt, and the Horn of Africa were to join the board. The other half of our Board consisted of "high net worth" individuals, plus a few clergy like me who had a reputation for raising funds among such people. Each year, for three days, the full Board would meet and vote on projects presented to us for consideration. The only ones who were permitted to vote were the Global South Primates, plus the President (Bishop Duncan) and the Chairman (me).

Beyond the remarkable privilege of meeting and spending time with these men who represented the very best of Anglicanism worldwide, came a feeling of doing something practical and much needed for the poorest of the poor. Our American board members reasoned that we in the West could not expect these bishops and archbishops to come to our aid over the theological and moral crises in our Episcopal Church and in the entire Anglican Communion without coming to their aid in the very practical needs that they were facing day to day. In our first three years, we raised nearly $3 million to fund some 75 projects around the globe. ARDF was off to a great start, and has continued to flourish, thank God. By now the total amount is well over $6 million raised for over 200 projects.

ARDF Board Meetings required me to jet off to various gatherings, which became a hallmark of my ministry. We met in locations where there were significant numbers of potential donors: Philadelphia, Pittsburgh, Vero Beach (Florida), Newport Beach (California), Dallas, Fort Worth, and Washington, D.C.

ALASKA

A second adventure that year was our family trip to Alaska. This was David's inspiration, thanks to his growing interest in photography. So, in the summer of 2005, Sandra, David, a friend of his from Stony Brook School where he was attending, and I flew to Anchorage, with the express purpose of photographing this last frontier of North America. I was frankly nervous. Not only did I assume that we would be cold, even though the month was July, but I was leery of one aspect of the trip: our time among the grizzly bears.

As it happened, we spent five nights in a campsite adjacent to the beach in Katmai National Park on the Alaskan Peninsula. We would be surrounded by grizzly bears. Our only protection was a couple of thin wires strung around the campsite, with two flashlight batteries for electrification. We encamped, buried all our food (for obvious reasons), and set up our defense. It worked. One night, a cub sniffing around the perimeter of our site touched the wire with its nose. We heard a yelp, and the little creature scampered up the hillside behind us. Eventually it tumbled down the steep incline into its mother's arms. But bear-lovers are known to have been eaten *in this very park* by these carnivorous animals, which usually weigh several hundred pounds, so I was not fully reconciled to our location. That lack of assurance was tested when, standing by myself, I saw two large grizzlies emerge out of the tall grasses a mere 50 yards away, headed in my direction. Fortunately, they were more interested in each other than in me, and they sauntered past. On another day I counted 15 grizzlies grazing within eyesight, one a mere 8 feet away, which gave me plenty of reason to feel a little queasy. This Alaskan adventure included whale watching, seeing Mt. McKinley on a clear day, and gaping at glaciers in Prince William Sound. As a trip, it was a huge success.

GRAND PARENTS

In early 2006, as we had each spring, we went to Hobe Sound, Florida to spend time at our favorite escape location: Jupiter Island. This year we managed to stay a bit longer. Sandra's parents, Audy and Fritz Clark, had added a charming guesthouse to their home on the

Intracoastal Waterway, and it was there over the years that we were welcomed for weeks at a time. It was staffed with the redoubtable Anita MacDonald, an Irishwoman with a penchant for work that would shame Hercules, and Mary McFadden, an African American who had become part of the family. The place was run like a cruise ship. Lunches at the Jupiter Island Club, tennis lessons, waterskiing, windsurfing (I kept a windsurfer in the garage), and in the early years, requisite trips to the Gardens Mall or Orlando's Disney World, were things eagerly looked forward to during our long northern winter months.

These annual trips also kept us in touch with a number of the grandparents of the young people we were trying to reach through FOCUS. The chaplains at the seasonal Christ Memorial Chapel on the island were more than hospitable to FOCUS. Each year they sponsored "youth chaplains" who would descend during Spring Break to build relationships with the young, most of whom attended northern boarding schools. These groups consisted of FOCUS staff and college-age assistants. In this way, the connection between the ministry I had founded and this semi-tropical retirement community was particularly satisfying. It was also exciting to see how the ministry at the Chapel had become more and more biblical, thanks to the faithful ministry of the Very Rev. Joel Pugh and The Rev. David Prior—both of whom effectively preached the Gospel.

THE FELLOWS INITIATIVE

The second entrepreneurial venture that I embarked upon during this first (and so far only) year of "retirement" was the creation of The Fellows Initiative. I had watched John Yates and his Falls Church in Virginia raise up a very effective fellows program for post college students. Then in its twelfth year, it was turning out some of Trinity Seminary's finest students, even though the goal of the program was to encourage "alumni" to serve God in secular callings. The formula they had hatched combined study, ministry, paid work, and mentoring, with the Fellows living in the homes of parishioners. I saw this as a brilliant way of bringing some of the brightest and best back into the life of vibrant parishes at precisely a time in their lives when many were casting about for clear guidance about their vocations.

I asked John and his team of workers if I could replicate the idea in other churches—essentially, "market" the fellows concept around the country. Two programs were already up and running, but other churches, including our own St. Stephen's in Sewickley, were eager to try the idea. With the encouragement of a $100,000 "goodbye present" from the Trinity Board of Trustees to help start The Fellows Initiative, and with the keen administrative insights of Becca Chapman, TFI was launched that fall. Becca carried the burden, and I provided encouragement and vision. Soon several churches were launching fellows programs, and I had the fun of teaching apologetics to our Pittsburgh Fellows who were based at St. Stephen's. Today TFI is a growing force across the country, bringing post -college students into church-based internship programs.

While teaching this course, I soon found myself walking side by side with some very fine young adults at a crucial juncture in their lives. Neil Rabi, Nate Harper, and Russell Johnston were only three of those to whom I drew close. But I continued to teach and mentor as I transitioned from my most active years administering various programs into my senior years when I was eager to pass on the Lord's wisdom to others.

MENTORING

Nate Harper was to become a special friend and colleague at this time. Although he was only the age of my children, he responded very well to an older man's friendship, and eventually invited me to "sponsor" him as he pursued life as a graduate student at Oxford and a missionary to the Arab world. In the summer of 2009, David and I joined three others for a tour of his adopted Arab country. Nate charted our way through busy souks, mountain trails, smelly fish markets, and conversations with Muslims eager to convert us to their way. The trip included two overnight stays in Dubai—the Las Vegas of the Middle East. There we gawked at enormous high rise buildings, indoor ski mountains, and endless shopping arcades while cooling ourselves in a vast swimming pool as a final refuge from the oppressive heat. In 2010, when Nate had decided to pursue Anglican ordination, he and I met in Cairo where I introduced him to Archbishop Mouneer Anis, the Bishop of Egypt and Archbishop of the Middle East. Before meeting the bishop, we managed to explore the wonders of Rhodes, Greece (on motor scooters), and drift down the Nile in a floating dormitory taking in many of Egypt's remarkable antiquities. When he finished his Oxford M.A. in 2012, he became my Sherpa, helping me with bags as we embarked on an extraordinary ten-day tour of Denmark, Sweden, Estonia, Finland, and Russia.

GLOBAL SEMINARIES

The third venture that I got involved in during the year I call my "faux sabbatical" was made possible by two grants of $5,000 each—one from a dear friend, and the other from the Episcopal Church. This money enabled me to visit Anglican theological seminaries worldwide in order to assess the strength of theological education, especially in the evangelical wing of the Anglican Communion. Thanks to these grants, Sandra and I flew to England and visited six seminaries there, and then we headed off for a fascinating tour of Uganda and Kenya.

I can still remember the surprise on Sandra's face when, in Uganda, she was asked (on several occasions) to "bring a word" to the assembled students and faculty. Despite her reticence to speak in public, she carried off the challenge with aplomb. Africans loved her, and she developed a taste for that Continent and a longing to reach out to some of its neediest that continued for years to come. On top of these adventures, we flew to Peru, Chile, Argentina, and Brazil, meeting students and clergy, and viewing seminaries in South America. A particularly memorable event was the visit to an Anglo-Chilean family in southern Chile who ran a sheep ranch two hours from nowhere. The endless stretches of what seemed uninhabited wasteland, with spectacular mountains and lakes in the distance, all ending with tea and crumpets in an English garden made us wonder where on earth we were.

CHAPTER 17

FOCUS REDUX

A SURPRISING INVITATION

As my one year of official retirement drew to a close, I received one of those "Ah ha!" phone calls that could not have been more unexpected. It was my brother-in-law, Peter Clark, asking if I would consider returning to FOCUS temporarily as Interim Executive Director. The call came just a half hour before I was to meet with Bishop Duncan and discuss the possibility of volunteering to be the Director of the Anglican Relief and Development Fund. Naturally, I was more than curious as to why FOCUS would ask its founder to come back after a hiatus of exactly twenty years. The reasons soon became clear: FOCUS was in financial trouble, and was experiencing other difficulties. Staff members were discouraged, and some regions had been without leadership for an unhealthy time. The Board was disunited. But the principal reason FOCUS took the unprecedented action of inviting me back was that it hoped I would be able to pull the ministry out of the financial doldrums.

RIP VAN WINKLE

My return to the ministry I had founded nearly 45 years earlier reminded me of the story of Rip Van Winkle, Washington Irving's famed character who returned from a deep sleep to discover that, in the twenty intervening years, America had won a Revolutionary War. Life at FOCUS therefore seemed in one sense familiar and in another strange. The ministry had grown from the ten staff with which I had left it in1985 to now well over forty. Its office had migrated from a large Sunday School room in Greenwich, Connecticut, to a swish corporate suite (which I discovered it could not afford) in Charlottesville, Virginia. The dedicated Woody Bowman and Richard Gwathmey were still hanging on as faithful long-term staffers, and the Study Center on Martha's Vineyard was still the vibrant center of summer operations—though now much expanded with the addition of several handsome buildings.

With the board's help, and with a great deal of prayer, I set about pursuing several goals. First, I would try to put the ministry back on a solid financial footing. With "hat in hand," I returned to many old friends who had supported the ministry and pled the special circumstances we were in. The response was enormously gratifying, for which I truly thank God. Second, I scoured the landscape for candidates for new leadership for those regions that were, or were soon-to-be, without present leadership: Florida, Raleigh, Washington, Baltimore, New Jersey, New York City, Hartford (the boarding school ministry), and Boston. From my initial survey, this seemed to be an almost total overhaul of senior leadership.

Despite my efforts, I was unable to locate an Area Director for New Jersey and the stellar candidate I did find for Florida, Scott Williams, was unable to raise sufficient funds to continue beyond one year. However, with some shuffling of positions around the

East Coast, and with the providential identification of several exceptionally fine new candidates, we were able to fill positions in Washington, Baltimore, New York City, Hartford, and Boston. Daria Kramer took over Washington, Andy McGovern Baltimore, Nathan Hart New York City, Rob Lofberg succeeded Cliff Swartz in the boarding school arena, and Dom Taylor came over from England to become our first Boston Director in several years. Each of these recruits warrants a story of his own, and "persuading" each to join this ministry had some humorous aspects to it. But once again, we proved the old adage: God does provide workers for his vineyard.

A HOUSE IN NATICK

Dom Taylor required the most extensive persuasion, in part because he had a great job as a reporter for a Formula One racing magazine. In the end he and Anna, his adventuresome wife, had a very deep call from God to join FOCUS. Recruiting them required me to spend a week in London that included shopping in Harrods, watching fireworks on Guy Fawkes Day, a black-tie FOCUS dinner at a very stuffy gentleman's club, observing Dom's rock group perform at an East End night club, and bedding down in a room barely big enough for a bed and my suitcase.

Leaving behind all that they knew to be "home" required some special treatment for Dom and Anna. Therefore, I purchased a house in Natick, Massachusetts, and had great fun recruiting all my younger friends to help fix it up so that it could be rented to them as a home and office for the freshly reconstituted Boston Area. Three years later, Dom, Anna and newly-born Arabella moved to the Southborough L'Abri community, and the house—now considerably gentrified—quickly sold. Sad to say, after several years of excellent work, the

Taylors felt called to return to England to work in the parallel ministry to our own based in the northern part of that country.

My third goal for this surprising return to FOCUS was to ensure the viability of the Study Center on Martha's Vineyard. Thanks to the CCCU, Council of Christian Colleges and Universities, one of their off-campus programs had entered into a contract to rent our facility from September through April. For several years they had brought college students to the wintry and often bleak Vineyard for fall and spring semesters, where students would learn to write and perform music. Because of the infusion of cash, the CCCU covered the carrying costs of our facility during the fall, winter and spring months, so that FOCUS was able to continue to improve its buildings, maintain a kitchen staff, and pay a year-round facilities manager. Our relationship with this important tenant, however, was unstable and needed some careful massaging. I built a friendship with their leaders, maintained a close watch over the process of contract writing, and made improvements on the buildings and grounds to meet their specifications. Here again, my own "beautification" skills came into play, and I couldn't resist clearing trees and brush so that the then-lost view of Seth's Pond was re-opened. I also killed poison ivy, and planted flowers and shrubs. In 2010, nonetheless, the CCCU moved their operation to the nation's music center: Nashville, Tennessee.

During what I call my Rip Van Winkle years, I never attempted to be involved in the program side of FOCUS, nor did I do much school visiting or work with parents and individual donors, other than to appear at various fund-raising events. I zeroed in on the key goals that I felt were of greatest importance, and left the rest of the ministry in the hands of our capable staff. This proved to be the right decision, although I did miss the opportunity to speak to students as

I had during the early years of FOCUS, and regretted the all-too-few opportunities I had to mentor up-and-coming leaders. I was thrilled when in 2008 the board handed over the reins of the ministry to Dan Walker, a seasoned man who had made his tentative first steps in Christ through FOCUS as a schoolboy and who had spent twelve years as one of our Area Directors. As a link in the chain of this apostolic succession, I had baptized a teenaged Dan many years before, after his conversion to Christ.

CHAPTER 18

CHARLESTON

HEADING SOUTH

An old friend, Louine King, put the news that Sandra and I had moved to Charleston, South Carolina this way: "the South finally got you, Peter." It made me smile, because I think she meant it to be flattering. After finishing my second tour of duty with FOCUS, I became an Associate minister at St. Michael's Church. A call from Al Zadig, a good friend and newly-ensconced Rector of St. Michael's, asked if there might be a way for Sandra and me to move to Charleston to help in this 260-year old parish. Al thought that my gifts and the needs in the parish (and City) might dovetail. Therefore, once I had bid my second good-bye to FOCUS, Sandra and I headed south to what—from many previous visits—I considered one of the most charming cities in North America.

After a two-month discernment, we decided to sell our Sewickley house, and move to South Carolina. Thanks to Sandra's remarkable real estate skills, the Sewickley house sold within a week of being offered, and just months prior to the housing bust of 2008. How fortunate we were because after we left, the house remained empty for nearly three years as the new owners found themselves unable to sell their current home.

FAMILY TIES

South Carolina turned out to be far from a crazy idea. Not only could we now, in our senior years, enjoy a milder climate (quite un-mild June through August however), but Sandra's grandfather had once owned a plantation in this State. During her childhood, Sandra had made many a happy trip there. Plus her cousin was married to a Charleston native, and her brother, Peter, was soon to move to Hilton Head, S.C. We were also now much closer to Audy Clark who was spending the full year in Florida, and my brother, Eric, lived in Western North Carolina. So it seemed that for the moment the family was gathering from the four corners—or at least we hoped so.

St. Michael's was just the right place for me. People opened their homes, and, more important, their hearts. My longing to preach, teach, and work with small groups could be amply fulfilled. The seeds of an exciting men's ministry were soon sown, and the special gift of many new and deep friendships in Christ added to the blessings.

NEW FRIENDS

We were exceptionally fortunate to find that our next-door neighbors, Stephen and Elizabeth Lenes and their four children, welcomed us. The house we rented was not only beautiful but well suited to our needs. It looked out on a charming manmade lake where swimming, kayaking, windsurfing and paddle boarding could all take place. Plus the community had a simple tennis and swimming club just blocks away from our house. We have since purchased a home nearby.

The Charleston part of my story, of course, continues as God's plan unfolds and as I move into the second half of my seventies, and God willing, beyond. With summers off to travel, to prepare for the fall, and to preach where invited, I am able to escape some of the worst of the Low Country's sultry heat. But air conditioning and ceiling fans make life not only bearable, but pleasant.

Of particular joy to me has been the ability to continue playing tennis—both singles and doubles. My redoubtable coach, Tiago Bruniera, had his faith in Christ revived through Alpha, and became a special friend, along with many other men in their twenties, thirties, and forties too numerous to name. One of these, Burwell Boykin, has helped me drive north from South Carolina on several occasions, acting as a de facto "chauffeur"—a title I enjoy bestowing on him as a tease for his blue-blood Southern background.

Thanks to Robby Marion and others I've continued the practice of taking men west for a week of winter sports. An annual ski trip to Vail and Beaver Creek has attracted a growing list of southern men, as well as northerners who like me have moved south and miss their annual adventure of schussing down some challenging trails.

As the years continue, it is a particular joy watching our three children mature and fulfill their own dreams. Fortunately, they seem to love to visit this historic and picturesque city, with its many charms. So we don't feel too separated, though we do wish they were nearer. In 2012 David married a wonderful young woman, Alexandra Egedy, and together they moved to Philadelphia. And Kate and Sean to our incredible joy have presented us with our first grandchild, Rhyan Mackay Norris. Jen has moved to Venice, California where she's successfully fulfilling a dream of establishing a wine-bar and restaurant. There, she is also able to be close to her special friend, Ric Krause. As occasion warrants, we parachute in to each of these locations for brief visits. And we all still manage to gather at key points in the year and celebrate our love even if only for a few days at a time

IN RETROSPECT

There are far too many lessons learned from this lifetime of family, travel, and above all ministry to recount. But here are just a few. First of all and most important, nothing compares with having a living relationship with Jesus Christ. What began for me as a teenager has continued throughout my life by the grace of God. Despite character faults all to evident to me, I never cease to be surprised that God really loves me. I know I am as needy as the next person of forgiveness, healing, and restoration. Frequent failures in my efforts to walk the walk have been graciously covered by the love of God. His offering of himself in the Cross to cover these sins and his triumph in the Resurrection are truly my life's one and only song.

I also believe that family is one of God's most precious gifts. Ever since the breakup of my parents' marriage, I've believed that an enduring marriage and a deep commitment to one's children is the foundation of a happy life. My many travels, most of which were brought on by the kind of work I was called to do, put strains on both marriage and family, and the longsuffering and patient endurance Sandra showed during my frequent, long absences is a cause for deep gratitude. Fortunately, I love travel, and ever since my teenage years when my bedroom room walls were festooned with travel posters from around the world, I've loved the mystique of visiting romantic and faraway places. I don't have a specified bucket list; but Asia, other than Hong Kong, and Southeast Asia are pretty unfamiliar to me. Almost all the rest of this good earth has been seen.

I also strongly believe that the Christian ministry ought to be fun. The kind of fun I am really referring to is not necessarily expensive, nor does it involve grand and glorious trips. It's closer at hand than most think. It's stopping to smell the roses. It's having a sport like tennis that does not require deep pockets. It's a bicycle ride in the park, a break in the midwinter to ski a local hill, a men's hiking trip in the mountains, learning to windsurf on a breezy lake, a coffee and muffin at a local breakfast shop, a bunch of daisies in a vase in the living room—these and a myriad of other small pleasures can make all the difference in life. We are meant for joy, and we can take joy in the delights of a life that is varied and expansive even if our main focus is ministry and other people.

ANGLICANISM

I am also thankful that I was raised an Anglican and remain one. Am I proud of Anglicanism as it is so often expressed? No. I am often ashamed of the lukewarm, revisionist, Gospel-avoiding posture of my denomination. The Episcopal Church, which was my first home, and from the age of 22 onwards my chosen venue for ministry, has listened to the siren call of secularism and, frankly, has lost its way. It will soon founder on the rocks of modernity, conformity, and permissiveness. But when I look at the worldwide Anglican family, stretching around the globe and back through the centuries including the the sixteenth century Reformation, the Wesleyan revivals, and so much more I see it as a marvelous community of worship, prayer, mission, and compassion. I am proud to belong to it, and bear its name. I believe that in Anglicanism's reformed catholicism lies the hidden secret of comprehensive Christianity: biblical, creedal, liturgical (though not ritualistic), missional, and above all God-centered. Wherever it has been ignited by the Holy Spirit and tethered to the authority of Scripture, Anglicanism has proven itself as a place where one can find new life and grow into Christ-likeness.

Let me also say something about money. I do not mean having money but giving money. Since my teen years I have tithed—10%

or more—of my income. In my early years, this caused the auditor from the IRS to raise an eyebrow when looking at the charitable contributions column in my 1040. But I believe that God's work, whether at home or abroad, requires money. As Bishop Stanway, Trinity's first dean, used to say: "The best guarantee of a fresh supply of money is the right use of what you already have." Sometimes in my ministries I have erred on the side of frugality when it comes to spending donated funds. But I believe that God's money must be handled very carefully. For example, I don't think that religious organizations (or churches) should go into debt in order to do God's work, other than for capital expenditures. "Pay as you go" has been my philosophy, and it has stood me in good stead. Thankfully, since Gospel work has always been paramount in my vision, people have supported the various projects with which I've been associated. Trinity's nearly $14 million capital campaign probably earned me a reputation as a fund-raiser. But, thankful as I am for that, I would much rather be thought of as a visionary who isn't afraid to ask for the funds to do God's work. My experience is that when people see a person with a clear vision and a track record of faithfulness, they give.

Being open to the unexpected is something else I've learned to accept as the surprising works of the Holy Spirit. So much of life is unpredictable. On several occasions I recall being asked to preach with hardly a moment's preparation. Someone dropped the ball, and I had to step in. On another, at a fairly large dinner party in Grosse Pointe, Michigan with mo-town notables like Henry Ford, Jr. and Roy Chapin President of American Motors present, my hostess suddenly announced that I would now speak to the group. What do you say when you are suddenly dropped down in the midst of some party and find yourself speaking to a noted journalist, author, politician, academic or billionaire? You remember that you are still speaking to a sinner like yourself, in need of the love of God in Jesus Christ.

Let me also say something about mentoring. The best sermon, I believe, is the one that is preached to just one person. I have been more than fortunate to learn from many good mentors, stretching back to my early days as a believer. Some of these people passed through my life for only short periods. Others like John Stott and Jim Packer, to name only two, were there for me again and again. Their example, and that of so many others, has fired me with enthusiasm to be a reliable mentor to many younger people. I've often said: "Every Timothy needs a Paul, and every Paul needs a Timothy." With a gift for friendship, especially with those younger than myself, I've been blessed to count innumerable young men (and some women) as truly dear friends. I've laughed with them, at times cried with them, and listened to innumerable struggles and a few victories. I would like to think that they are my "letter of recommendation" before God and God's people, just as Paul saw his converts in Corinth to be his.

Finally, I believe that we should make an effort to continue to read and study throughout life, whether in a degree program like the Doctor of Ministry I started at the age of 50, or the reading I try to do, year in and year out. But like a lake that has only an inlet and no outlet, I also believe that those of us who've been taught how to speak and write should use our pens (or computers) to produce written material that applies the Gospel to the issues of our day. The books that I've written or edited, the book chapters I've contributed, and the booklets, newspaper editorials, magazine articles, and videos that I've put out all flow from a deep conviction that only a message shared is a message truly believed.

APPENDIX

"Owed to FOCUS by Charles Drew"
With apologies to Edgar Allen Poe
presented to Peter Moore on the occasion of
FOCUS's 50th Anniversary
September 24, 2011
Harvard Club
New York City

Once upon a midnight dreary,
while in Cambridge, weak and weary,
Pond'ring many a strained and spurious volume
of theological lore,
A young man nodded, nearly napping,
when suddenly there came a tapping,
As of some one gently rapping, rapping, at his
heart strings door.
"'Tis the Holy Ghost," he muttered, "tapping at
my heart string's door."
"Save the preppies ever more."

Startled he sat up and pondered. "Could it be,"
he prayed and wondered,
"That the faith so often sundered
from the founder's dreams of yore,
Could with freshness rise in rich kids? Could we
find a way to pitch kids?

Could there be a way to pitch kids while avoiding
all-out war?"
Surely there must be a way to pitch kids while
avoiding war."
"Woo the preppies, Peter Moore!"

Off to Oxford then for study, where faith-filled
Brits in fulsome flood he
Met and watched and studied under, building up
a mighty store.
Many souls, John Stott among them, spoke of
camps and often sung them,
Camps called "Bash" that had firmly swung them
joyful to the gospel's shore.
Could it be such camps might work way back at
home on U.S. shore?
"Dream your dreams, now, Peter Moore!"

Armed with hope and budding vision, Peter made
the grand decision
Risking loss and world derision, set himself to
work full-bore.
Things of course required some changing, U.S.
views of women ranging
Far beyond the celibacy that the stolid Brits
adore?
Should he move beyond the range, the range the
stolid Brits adore?
"Bring the girls in, Peter Moore!"

So bring them in he did with gusto, teaching all
to watch for lust, or
Making dear the marriage state, so good for sex
and much much more.
Then, the ever faithful leader, Pete to Sandy
raised his need, her

Life to join with his in union, come what may
from heaven's store?
Should all others join in union, come what may
from heaven's store?
Sound the nuptials, Peter Moore!!

Somewhere came the task of naming: how to
posture things by framing
Vision with a suited title that would cause kids to
explore.
CRIS explained it but was taken, UPSC was new
but could hardly 'waken,
FOCUS proved an able label, hard for seekers to
ignore?
Would FOCUS prove an able label, hard for
seekers to ignore?
Pitch the preppies, ever more!

But of course, the mighty selling came from love
and wit in telling
Ancient truths in terms that drew young hearts
to ponder and explore.
Skeptics came because of skiing; laughter, skits
and ways of seeing.
Ways of seeing and of being they had never met before.
Yes, there were new ways of being they had
never met before.
So came preppies, more and more.

Where to meet for all this learning? Peter
thought with deepened yearning.
Where to get young hearts away to think and
talk and pray and roar.
Carol Lodge? Or maybe Pawling? Ledges Grey?
They all were calling.
None proved terribly enthralling…Then, lo, a call

from Martha's shore.
Could there be a home for FOCUS, beckoning
from Martha's shore?
To the Vineyard, Peter Moore!

Poison ivy clung to claim him, breaking barn
beams sought to maim him,
Weary staff arose to blame him, Still he toiled,
did Peter Moore
So to make that place a haven
(Preppie souls, they needed savin'!)
'Till at last the vision took on form we happily adore
Does that place define a vision that we happily adore?
Yes, indeedy, Peter Moore.

Friendships, marriages abounding,
fulsome laughter, joy astounding.
Finding Christ and in Him grounding
all our hopes for life's full store.
Filling churches with new preachers,
filling schools with ardent teachers
Keen to see the reign of Jesus fill the earth from
shore to shore.
This and more we owe to FOCUS, love and truth
from shore to shore.
God be praised for ever more.

September 24, 2011

INDEX

BIOGRAPHY: PETER C. MOORE

Born and raised in suburban New York City, Peter attended public schools through the 8th grade and then went to St. Mark's School in Massachusetts from which he graduated in '54. After 4 years at Yale, he attended Jesus College, Oxford and got his M.A. in theology, finishing his theological studies at E.T.S. in Cambridge, Mass. in '61.

Peter then served as vicar of an industrial parish outside of Pittsburgh for 2 years before becoming the Director of the Council for Religion in Independent Schools in N.Y.C. At the same time he started FOCUS, Inc. a ministry to private secondary schools in New England that has expanded over the next 50 years to involve 30 staff in 10 regions from Boston to North Carolina. FOCUS touches hundreds of students weekly in scores independent secondary schools. Also Peter and his wife Sandra developed a beautiful conference facility for the FOCUS ministry on Martha's Vineyard Island, Mass.

Peter left FOCUS in 1985 and became Rector of "Little" Trinity Anglican Church, Toronto, where he, his wife, Sandra, and their three children lived for a decade. While there he received his Doctor of Ministry from Fuller Seminary.

In 1996 Peter became the fourth Dean and President of Trinity Episcopal School for Ministry in Ambridge, PA. While there he completed a capital campaign that raised $14 million for the seminary.

Retiring in 2004, Peter became Chairman of Anglican Relief and Development Fund, and began The Fellows Initiative based in Sewickley, PA. – an organization helping large churches establish internship programs for post-college students. In 2005 he was asked by the Board of FOCUS to return as (interim) Executive Director. He served as FOCUS Director from 2005 to 2008.

During the summer of 2008 he and Sandra moved to South Carolina where he became Associate for Discipleship at St. Michael's Church in downtown Charleston. They have three grown children.

Peter is the author of four books, and editor of two others. He received an honorary Doctor of Divinity from Nashotah house in '03.

Edwards Brothers Malloy
Thorofare, NJ USA
August 29, 2013